REQUIEM

KM Bailey

Copyright © 2025 KM Bailey

All rights reserved

The characters and events portrayed in this book are fictitious. Any similarity to real persons, living or dead, is coincidental and not intended by the author.

No part of this book may be reproduced, or stored in a retrieval system, or transmitted in any form or by any means, electronic, mechanical, photocopying, recording, or otherwise, without express written permission of the publisher.

ISBN: 9798319073822

Cover design by: Art Painter
Library of Congress Control Number: 2018675309
Printed in the United States of America

For Dad, who was a generous and kind man.

CONTENTS

Title Page
Copyright
Dedication
Historical Note

CHAPTER 1	1
CHAPTER 2	9
CHAPTER 3	17
CHAPTER 4	26
CHAPTER 5	28
CHAPTER 6	42
CHAPTER 7	48
CHAPTER 8	53
CHAPTER 9	60
CHAPTER 10	68
CHAPTER 11	74
CHAPTER 12	80
CHAPTER 13	87

CHAPTER 14	93
CHAPTER 15	96
CHAPTER 16	104
CHAPTER 17	109
CHAPTER 18	119
CHAPTER 19	129
CHAPTER 20	133
CHAPTER 21	137
CHAPTER 22	152
CHAPTER 23	163
CHAPTER 24	170
CHAPTER 25	177
CHAPTER 26	181
CHAPTER 27	185
CHAPTER 28	191
CHAPTER 29	201
CHAPTER 30	207
CHAPTER 31	214
CHAPTER 32	223
CHAPTER 33	229
CHAPTER 34	241
CHAPTER 35	247
CHAPTER 36	254
CHAPTER 37	264

CHAPTER 38	267
CHAPTER 39	273
CHAPTER 40	280
CHAPTER 41	285
CHAPTER 42	295
CHAPTER 43	301
CHAPTER 44	305
CHAPTER 45	311
CHAPTER 46	314
CHAPTER 47	317
CHAPTER 48	321
1939	334
CHAPTER 49	335
CHAPTER 50	340
About The Author	343

HISTORICAL NOTE

There were nearly 900,000 British Military fatalities during the Great War, with many more returning from the front with life altering injuries, but more tragedy was to follow. In the last summer of the war Spanish Flu had started to spread, reaching the shores of Britain. A quarter of the population were affected and over 200,000 people died.

NOTE ON COMPOSITION

My book is written in UK English. Differences in the spelling of certain words and in the grammatical construction of sentences may be due to language and cultural differences.

CHAPTER 1

LETTERS

Tom

Seventy days on the frontline, a long stint – but I know we are nearing the end of it. Any day now we'll be called back. The war is over. Who won? – not us. Not them. We did – Tommy. My name is Tom. Tom Baxter. I've been in this trench for seventy days – did I say? My luck held. I dodged the gas and the snipers popping, the shrapnel and the shells. Reckon I'll get back home any day now – any day now.

Last night we slept in the dugout, lying with our legs knitted one over another and dozens of rats with heads as big as rabbits crawling amongst us, biting holes in our haversacks to get at our rations. I'm used to them now, but some men can't stand them, and you can't kill them, see – there's no point, they breed like bloody rabbits. Doug Carsten says each pair of rats can make nine hundred more – imagine that – so there's no point in bashing them with the butt of your rifle, waste of puff, he says.

My boots leaked ever since I got them, never mind the puttees. Some days the mud sloshed over our thighs and seeped in both ends. God, I hate the mud. Brown, black, thick, bloody mud – sometimes in nightmares I thought I'd drown in it, but I didn't.

An hour before dawn the company orderly, he's a stubby runt of a man, and Sergeant Mathers go along the line kicking us awake and it starts again. We climb up on the fire-step one last time, bayonets fixed and stick our heads up ready. We're so close to the end now, but there's still time for one of us to get it in the head. But there's no dawn raid. Bloody hell there's no-one there – they must have upped sticks and scarpered in the night. Carsten's laughing, tears rolling down his mug and the Sergeant bawls him out, but we're all laughing now.

Day seventy-five. We don't all make it out the trench o' course. Some men are too far gone, no fight left to get away – away from the reek of cordite and piss. Did I say? – war smells real bad – mud smells bad; creosol, woodbines, dead men not yet picked up for burial not ten yards from the trench, even the rotting sandbags stink and when did Tommy last have a bath?!

Another month has come and gone and we're still waiting. They got us here quick enough to fight but getting us back's another thing. Turns out those who've been here longest get to go first, them and the officers. All we want to do is get home, but no, there's this and that to do and we're stuck on the coast of France waiting for the army to give us our papers to get back home. I'll not be back for Christmas Mum – this rate I'll not be back for next Christmas.

Three months pass and at last I get my ticket home. Finally, I'm on board, and we're all rammed in thick as in the trenches. All dead beat, broken, some still not free from where they've been – you can see it in their eyes – they'll be no good when they get back. I sleep – the sleep of the dead my mum would say.

On reaching London I'm given three letters, one just a few weeks old, the other a few months and the third has been waiting for me for nigh on two years. The second letter is from my mother, I recognise her hand and I read this one first.

16th January 1919, Long Wendon
Dearest Tom,

I hope that you are home soon. Christmas has come and gone and still no word of you. Rose and Will miss their big brother so, and I had hoped to see you before the winter was past. There is work for you here, son, for I know it is hard to find for soldiers coming back from the war. You are to have work in the grounds at Grange Park, now your father is gone, and I thank the master for it, for he has been so kind to us.

When this letter finds you son, and I hope it is soon, I would ask a promise of you. It is not so very much Tom, only what you would do of your own free will if you were here now. I would ask that you always take good care of your brother and sister.

Your loving Mum,
Lilian Baxter

It is a strange kind of letter for her to write me. She is not one for sending letters, though I know she worries, but that's just on account of her not knowing so well how to write the words. I guess she must have had Susan help her – I'll mind to ask my sister when I'm back. It is a sad and cheerful letter, and I cannot figure it straight. But this letter is not so hard in the end, for it is the next two that set my head spinning.

I am on the train, the wheels turn, but I can't close my eyes, though it's bringing me home. To what? Another letter is in my hand, but I don't know how it makes me feel. The letter is from Reverend Hawkins, our parish priest, written on the third of March, just a few weeks past. It tells me my mother is gone – that the Spanish flu has taken her off. Then there's something about Will, we call him Billy, and Rose and what has become of them, and lastly the letter tells me to return home with God's speed so that business can be settled. Poor Mum, she stayed alive through this long war, but not long enough to see me home.

Dad has been dead these two years, Susan, my eldest sister is wed, and that just leaves me and Rose and Billy. They're mine now, to look out for, but all I want to do is run. I heard you could get to Canada or Australia maybe and that's where I was headed, soon as I could. I'd be back long enough to say my goodbyes and then I'd go – use some of my back pay to get a passage, maybe even work some of it and give the rest to Mum to help out see. She had a job at the big house, she was doing all right, there was a roof for them to stay under, but now what? I'm not wanting to step into my father's shoes. Mum wrote me to say Dad was dead and the army regretted his loss… But I know the truth of it now. I have this last letter in my hand.

The Reverend Henry White, a serving army chaplain has written it. And I know the truth of it, the shame of it and the half-truth of it. Here's what he wrote me and I hate him for it. I hate his kindness; I wish he'd left it alone. I wish I didn't know.

19th December 1919, Flers, Haut de France

Dear Private Thomas Baxter,

I am writing to you, as I feel I must, for I was witness to this act, and should it come to light later then it is best that you should know the truth from me and no-one else. Several months have passed while I have sought to find you, knowing from your own good pastor the Reverend Hawkins that you have been this long time at the war.

There is no easy way for me to impart this to you and I deeply regret that this news should reach you by way of a letter, but in these times, there is no other way. Your father has been found guilty by military court and has been executed for the crime of desertion. I know this will come as a great shock to you and I can only mitigate this news by expressing my profound sorrow at this outcome and affirming my unwavering belief that a grave error has been made.

Your father was attended by a medical man, Dr Ian Glenister, before his court martial who found him to be much changed in his disposition. As a soldier yourself you will have seen what this war has done to many men. Your father was thus affected, and the opinion of the good doctor was that his condition warranted a prolonged absence in order to become whole in body and mind and fit once more for duty. The court neither heard nor headed this advice for no defence was sought and it is to their shame.

I spoke with your father at length after he was sentenced, and such was his altered state of mind that truly he had no fear of what was about to befall him. He was, I would say, even childish in his faith that this was a 'to-do' that would be quickly remedied. In those brief hours I found him to be a most honourable man.

I sincerely offer my condolences and trust in God that your father is now at peace, and moreover I trust that you and your family will not be brought to suffer through this senseless and unnecessary act.

Yours in faith and pity,
The Reverend Henry C. White

I stuff the letter back in my pack and close my eyes. My heart thumps heavily inside me and still I can't sleep. Rage keeps the tears locked down inside me. Dad? When I think on him now, I can't find answers to the things this letter doesn't say. There is no how or why to any of it. It's not how I knew him, it's not the same man. I always knew him brave. The only thing he was ever afraid of was a stupid thing and that was rats – and that was a great laugh to us all – a man born to the land and afraid of a rat! Sure, I've seen men I know set to wander, the light gone out in their eyes, like they was walking in their dreams, but not our dad! Could he have wandered away like those lost men I saw? No – I can't see him like that. I can't – it's not my dad.

CHAPTER 2

1913

Tom

"Rose, Rose, mind Will!" shouts Mum as Billy runs to get out the door before she can catch him and put clean clothes on him.

"No you don't Billy Baxter," laughs Rose as she grabs hold of her brother and swings him up in the air. Billy laughs – he wants to run and Rose wants to chase him and I can see Susan is going to get real mad, real soon and slap them both.

"Mum, Mum, they'll ruin my skirt. Rose keeps running into the chair and she's kicking up the dirt and she'll knock over the bowl," shouts Susan.

"There's no dirt on my floor Susan Baxter, and I'll thank you not to say there is. We may be plain folk, but we keep a tidy home and never you let your father hear you say otherwise." That's always what Mum says, and according to Dad she can't be wrong.

I'm sixteen tomorrow, Billy's three and Rose, pretty Rose, was eight last month. Susan, my eldest sister, is eighteen and gets married today and it can't be soon enough for me. She's got airs my sister, but she won't be so high and mighty when she's running after a brood of her own. Me? I want to go places; I want to see the world. No girl will catch me and make me put a ring on her finger – least not before I've been to sea and seen all the places on the map. I've two years to wait. Dad says that I need to stay and work here while the little 'uns are still little and help the family before I go. But when I'm eighteen, that's me, I'm off.

We're working folk, but not dirt poor like the Clarks. My wages help some when there's work to be got but it's not regular like. It's long and hard – another reason I've a hankering to go. We've got this house that Dad rents from our landlord – Sir Peter Mountfield – we're a bit rammed in, what with just the two rooms but there's only the six of us and Susan'll be gone tonight. Dad's got skills with his hands – he's the cobbler here in the village. He learnt his trade in Bedford, years past and it gives our family a living. It's hard work mind, he goes from place to place collecting shoes and boots to mend and then sits in his hut out the back 'til all hours fixing and teasing the old things back to use. Then he has to deliver them back, slings the laces over the front of his bicycle and pedals them back. Sometimes I would go on his bicycle after school, it was fine in the summer, when I could fly through the lanes, see, my feet just touching the pedals, but in winter when the lanes were dark you had to go real slow or you'd most like crash into someone walking the other way. Mum didn't like me going out in the winter darkness, but that's when Dad was busiest, that's just when people's shoes got wore out most.

I liked it best when he had an order for new boots or shoes, we'd sit and watch him cut the new leather and it smelt good. He'd get more for those of course and maybe that would mean Mum would make a fine pudding with more than two pennyworths of bits to fill it out.

Here? Here is called Long Wendon and it's like any of twenty villages in the county. The houses are all dotted about, like they've sprung up from the ground. Maybe they have. The landlord's added to them over the time we've been here, but they're all, every one of them, knocked about looking. Nothing smart, but they're fit to live in, not like the ones out beyond Broomfield. The landlord's meant to fix and patch the roofs and the like, and he does every now and then, so we're not so bad. They say the landlord's soft, but the overseer – not a chance – you pay in advance, or you get two weeks' notice. Then you're out. Most times folk try to help each other out when work dries up for a neighbour – see them through to their next wage day when it comes. But when there's a poor harvest or the work's scarce for all it's hard and then someone has to leave. That's just the way of it.

When I say it's a village, it's quite a big place, bigger than Broomfield, though it's in the countryside and there's no factories or the like or anything like that. We're country folk, farmers and labourers and there are plenty of farms round about for us to work on.

There's a shop in the village – Oram's – that's where the nearest outside tap to us is. Every day before school I'd go and get the water for Mum. Now I'm left, it's Rose's job and she takes an age and is most times late for school, being only little. Washday is Monday, and Mum would never let us wear anything that was dirty, so we need lots of water. Out the back of the cottages there's coppers in the barns that the whole village use. Washing takes all day and of course Susan helps, she's got day work at the house but not on Mondays. That's where she met her man. She's a maid there and he's the son of the overseer and he works on the estate. He's a step up from us so Susan's done well for herself, though he's ten years older in age.

You can get most things in the village; Mum keeps account of the shillings. Meat and eggs and the like are delivered to the door once a week.

There's a man here that catches sparrows and Mum usually gets a plate of them for two pence when he calls. She can make a good pudding out of a plate of sparrows. When it's harvest time, we lads stand ready with our sticks to catch the rabbits when they run out. Sometimes I've got lucky and I've caught one and Mum makes a fine pie out of it. There's not much money to go around, but that's the same for everyone. We get by on what there is and what we can find. I've lived here all my life, it's what it is, but I want to go places, see more and I will.

My folk? Well, there's not many of us – just Mum, Dad and the four of us. My Mum's mum and dad are both dead and the rest of Mum's family are a long way off. We don't see them and they don't see us. Dad – well – I reckon there is no-one on his side of the family, leastways he never speaks of any.

My Mum's name's Lily, but Dad just calls her Mum like us. She's strict with us, but she loves us I know. Folk say she's kind to her neighbours and she keeps a neat house. Susan and I have both got the look of her. We've fair hair, blue eyes and pale skin, not like Billy and Rose and Dad – they've got jet, black hair and black eyes to match. They say my sister Rose will be a beauty when she's grown. I think Susan's jealous coz she always says no good will come of a working man's daughter looking like that. But not Mum – she says, 'God gave her that pretty face and he'll have had a reason.' I guess the reason's not found her yet, but it will.

Dad's a quiet man, but you don't want to get on the wrong side of him. I've done that in the past and I've regretted it. Did I say? His name's my name too – Tom. Mum says he works hard for us, and now I work too I know the truth of it. He gets up at dawn and often comes home late if he's got a delivery. People need their boots and shoes for work, so he tries to finish those he's got and get them back to folk as soon as he can. It's Saturday today, and we're waiting for Dad to come home and then Susan will be wed and life will go on as it always has.

As the time crawls past Susan frets more and no matter how many times Mum says she'll not be late for the church, Susan won't mind her. At last Dad comes through the door and Susan starts right in on him, but he stops her with a look, he has that trick to calm her, always had. I'm right glad Dad is home, for Susan in a fret makes everyone's mood black.

Dad is in no hurry of course. He sits himself down at the kitchen table and Mum takes his jacket from him. Billy, with the help of Rose brings Dad a cup of water and he spills most of it on the way across the room, but Dad don't mind. He smiles at Billy, takes the cup and drinks the little that is left, making a great show of it. Billy's lit up with it.

This little practice over, Dad goes outside to where Mum has set a bucket of water for him to wash in. He strips down to his waist and scrubs with a cloth and the cold water from the pail. He's a broad man my father, but you can see the skin stretched tight across his back, no flesh to spare on him. He comes back into the room and Mum hands him a clean shirt and at last we're ready to get my sister wed.

Dad offers his arm to Susan, and she hooks hers into it and we go outside.

Inside the church, our friends and neighbours are all gathered, and it seems to take just a little time before Susan and her man, Michael Crawley are married. There's plenty of dancing afterwards of course, with folk all bringing their fiddles and such like and for once there's plenty of food to go around. Everyone brings something and we share what we have with our neighbours. The harvest is in and so no-one needs to wake early, for though it's Sunday tomorrow, we would all be at work if there was still the harvest to bring home. So, there's only the Reverend Hawkins to upset if we don't make it to church in the morning, and by the look of things he's supping more that his fair share of the beer. The men all drink too much of course, and I'm lightheaded. Billy and Rose dance about with the village children, my little sister a dark headed angel in her Sunday frock as she goes cantering around to the tunes.

CHAPTER 3

LOOKING TO THE PAST

William

It has taken many years for me to find my voice and it has changed so many times during my life that sometimes I wonder that it is my voice at all. Until I was seven years old, I spoke like everyone else in our village, when of course I did speak, which was not often. It has always been one of my peculiarities, if I did not think there was anything of value to say then I simply would not say it. I don't remember when first I came to this strange realisation, but it must have been later rather than sooner, for those about me remembered my voice when I had it and then remembered when it was gone.

My name is Will Baxter, but sometimes I have been Billy and at other times William. I have no preference, for all these names have served me well and all these names have been dear to those who have used them at one time or another.

It is 1939 and the war has begun. I have been through basic training, though I know that the skills I will need for my part in the coming conflict are long learned – the skills to heal. I have been a doctor in general practice for nearly five years, and now I must test my knowledge in a field hospital in France, though I know the medicine I will practice there will be far removed from the sore throats, warts and measles of home. I am under no illusion that for the duration of this fight my arms will stay greased with the blood of the wounded and the dying. I was not so young during the Great War to not know where I am headed.

My circumstances are different to those of my father and brother who went before me. I've enlisted in the Royal Army Medical Corps and I am of officer class, though that was not what I was born to. How did I get here? I am a working man's son, bred into the rural life of my forbears who lived and died in this same, small Bedfordshire village where I was born. Back then I was Will to my mother and Billy to the rest of my family. When I was seven I became mute, and in the intervening years between then and now my voice was broken, its notes changed, and through the power of learning – a miracle that still humbles me – I became what I am now. Now I am William Baxter, and I am no better no worse for it – at heart I am the same.

From the age of 10 when I became William, I had little chance for reflection, my life racing into the future at full pelt, little time to stop and think too deeply of all things dead and gone. But now, as the train slowly pulls away from the station, away from my family, my wife, my children, alone in my thoughts for the first time in many years, now finally I can see clearly like a map laid out before me the how of it, the how of why I am.

I will begin at the beginning, although many of these memories, are not mine – for I was not yet born – but I can swear on my life that they are accurate. Back then, everyone knew everyone else's business and although the dividing line between the rich and the common folk was clearly marked, my class knew everything about the world of the rich, though I swear they were indifferent to ours. After all it was our entertainment and diversion from the grind of work and living to make supposition and comment about others' lives – we gossiped about our friends and neighbours, so why not about the rich folk on the hill?

Of course, the village knew all there was to know about Esther Mountfield. To our class she was not just the lady from the grand house who spread her largesse amongst the deserving poor, she was also the pitied wife of a neglectful husband. Esther, was in her fifties when I first came to gaze upon her, but even then, she was improbably blonde and very, very beautiful, but she was also hollow. She had given her husband, the lordly Sir Peter Mountfield, three fine sons, but as they grew into robust young men, she seemed to disappear in their lengthening shadows and began to diminish in her husband's eyes. His cruelty was casual, not intended, at least that's what the village said. But Esther was stronger than any gave her credit for, rather than crumbling into the oblivion of a neglected spouse, she diverted her passion and became instead a champion of the poor. The village even speculated that she would join the Suffragette movement, but only well out of ear-shot of her husband, for perhaps she was not that brave.

My sister Rose was to become one of Esther Mountfield's projects, but there were others too, though my sister being fair, gained a lion's portion of the good lady's benevolence. It was one of her peculiar prejudices – a subtle, invidious distaste for the plain children of the parish and it was a prejudice that brooked no real explanation. It was almost as if she were saying that if she could not see the beauty writ large in the face, then there was no worth to the body or soul. It was an irrationality that to her credit she recognised, many in her position would have simply followed their whim, and bestowed their kindnesses on those whom their fancies chose.

But Esther Mountfield ultimately had a good heart and as such forced herself to treat kindly wherever it was truly deserved. Nevertheless, those who were plain of face often found that her benefits took them away from the parish to start new lives as apprentices in trades the length and breadth of England. Her other kindnesses were often more generally applied in the form of donations of books to the schoolhouse and such like. But for those who were esteemed both worthy and handsome there was preferential treatment and those she would keep close – like a butterfly collection of the prettiest wings, these beautiful children were her passion and some would say her solace and escape from the lonely world her life with Sir Peter had now become. My sister Rose was very, very pretty, perhaps the fairest butterfly of them all.

But I digress, I said I would start at the beginning and here I am racing towards the middle before I have yet begun.

So, Esther Mountfield had three sons. The eldest was Edward, a tall, dark handsome man straight out of a novel. He was not arrogant or vain, merely a product of his class, a class that held itself superior as a birthright, a class yet to be challenged, a class that had persisted quite nicely thank you through generations of Mountfield heirs. He was at Oxford studying the law, perhaps more studious than his younger brothers and certainly less frivolous, but still carefree, young, and born to a life apart from the common man.

The next brother was named Peter after his father and had inherited his nature as well as his name; he wore an air of aristocratic arrogance about him as if it were a cloak. He was the tallest of the three and there was a self-assured ease about him that often went with being a second child. Peter was about to join his eldest brother at Oxford and would, for want of a better idea on his part, be reading law. Peter was not sure why he needed a profession, but it's what his class did and of course he was eager to indulge in the Oxford life that he knew Edward already enjoyed.

The third son was Arthur and he was still at school, but of the three he was the most gregarious and outgoing of the brothers. When his older siblings held parties at the family home, Grange Park, it was Arthur who delighted in them the most, indulging in all the pleasures that his nearly adult status afforded him. Their mother and father would often absent themselves on such occasions and Arthur would make the most of this lack of parental concern, not being one to heed the word of an older brother.

My sister, Susan, with disapproving regard for the sons of her employers would give clipped reports of their excesses, but far from inducing the response from her little sister that she had hoped, Rose would linger on the edited tales her more prudish older sibling would spin, dreaming it all in like a kitten filled up with cream from the dairy. She was delighted by the world around her in all its wondrous and varied forms and was eager to see the fine ladies and gentlemen of whom her sister had on many a past occasion spoken so censoriously.

It was the Spring of 1914 and there was again to be a ball at Grange Park. All the fine young things from the district had been invited and Edward was down from Oxford for the Easter break, bringing with him an assortment of his university friends. Rose was desperate to see the silks and the pearls and the partying and with her friend Maude, who was nearly eleven, she had plotted to slip away after bedtime and take a peek in at the windows.

This would be a daring trip, for the house was a good mile away from the village, but Rose was bold for her age and with her friend Maude the pair were fearless of the night. For them, the dark black skies held no terrors, just endless adventures to be lived. I still to this day don't know how she didn't get caught, but I have always suspected that our mother knew full well where she was headed when she slipped out the door. Perhaps she knew that Rose would keep to the shadows and would not be found out as she spied upon her elders and betters, or perhaps after all she did not hear the light footfall as Rose unlatched the door and ran away into the night and up the hill to the big house.

The next day, though her eyes bellied her lack of sleep, I heard her in thick whispers with Maude on the way to church, though at four years old it meant little to me, there was no mistaking their excitement and pleasure. I could picture their two small faces from the night before pressed against the glass, lost in their description of satin pumps and shimmering dresses with long fringes. Their talk was all of the women, the men did not feature large in their view, for they were drab creatures compared to the society girls with their blonde straightened hair and the brunettes with cropped black mops held back with jewelled pins or a single ribbon. They spoke of the fast feet of the ladies as they took to the dance floor, the men lounging with collars and shirts disarrayed and loosened as the night went on, and the heady music and the curls of cigarette smoke so exotic to their young eyes as it drifted upwards in Indian rings.

They giggled as they recounted how Arthur had spotted them, and how he had merely winked at them and then turned away. That of course had set them running back towards the village in a fright, lest he should give them away, with only the pale moonlight to lead them home.

As I look back to that spring Sunday of 1914,

it seems as if it existed in another time, a time of lightness that has long since vanished from memory.

CHAPTER 4

WAR

William

On the fourth of August 1914 the German army marched into Belgium and that night Britain entered the war. This announcement, far from engendering a sense of foreboding was met with rapturous applause from the crowds, for on that first day the nation was as innocent as I – a four-year-old child staring into the sky hoping to catch the fledgling glimpse of a shiny aeroplane crossing the path of the sun.

Three days later Lord Kitchener asked for a hundred thousand men to stand forth and proud and within days a hundred thousand men had attested their willingness to fight for King and Country. Within the year two million more had swelled the ranks of the British Expeditionary Force beyond all recognition, but not before time. Before that first year had turned most of the original force were dead, lost or wounded. Closer to home the army took the fathers of my friends, my own father and brother to its ranks, as well as the two eldest Mountfield boys and then later the youngest, Arthur.

Peter Mountfield broke his father's heart when he did not come back from the battle of the Somme in 1916. And as for Edward and Arthur? Arthur joined up the week after his brother died and rode out the remaining years of the war untouched. Edward did not return unscathed: a gas and mortar attack left him blind in the right eye. He was sent back home to England to convalesce. With reduced mobility and damage to his lungs so severe that evermore he would require the use of a cane to get around, he did not return to the field of war. I was eight when the war came to an end.

CHAPTER 5

THE PIANOFORTE

William

The school in Long Wendon was small by the standards of the day, with yearly attendance rarely reaching to forty pupils. In consequence, boys and girls were not segregated into different classes as was the norm of the time, neither were there separate entrances in the small stout building though boys' and girls' desks were set apart on opposite sides of the cramped room. It was poorly upkept, relying heavily on the church for much needed funds and indeed the Reverend Hawkins would often teach the older boys during the afternoon session, while the village school mistress, Eliza Adam remained in charge of the infants and older girls teaching basic arithmetic, reading and writing. Truth be told, though children were by law meant to attend between the ages of five and thirteen years, absences were high, as the children were often needed to work alongside their parents.

It was a great day in the village when the pianoforte arrived at the school. Brought on the back of a cart, a splendid polished wooden box, precariously perched on top of John Graham's dairy cart and tied with ropes. As it made its way down the rutted main street, it seemed to come to life with every jolt in the road and eerie chords sang out from its heart.

It was 1913 and I was three years old and not yet at school, but even so I was old enough to be fiercely envious of my sister Rose, as she had been picked as one of the privileged few who would be allowed to touch this wonderful musical contraption. She would get to trail her fingers softly over the notes and make them sing to her.

"It's not fair" I wailed, even now I remember the stinging inequality of it. "Why can't I play the lovely box?"

"It's not a box, Billy, don't be silly. It's a piano and…" Rose would always try to soothe my childish anger… "you will, you will! I know you will. But first you have to go to school, Billy," she said earnestly. "Then I'm sure the Mrs Lady will let you play. I know she will. When she sees how much you want to, she will for sure. She likes us to really want it, so I'm sure you will."

Of course, the problem with the piano when it first arrived was that no-one could play it. Miss Adam had been so overwhelmed by Lady

Mountfield's generosity that it had not occurred to her to confess that she could not teach her charges to play until after the instrument had arrived. This, however, to the great lady was not an insurmountable problem. She would not of course countenance herself teaching the children, though she possessed quite a considerable skill, that would have been too much for her husband, but she did have the means to employ a tutor from London. So once a week Mr Scrivens visited the school precisely at 9 o'clock and would leave at 3pm on the dot. Mr Scrivens did not inspire the children in either his looks or demeanour, being a dry stick of a man in his late thirties and they regarded him with suspicion and not a little fear to begin with. However, it soon became apparent that his was a magnificent gift, once he set his fingers to the keys his cold, nervous and stern exterior would disappear as the music flowed from his able finger tips. The children were entranced and a good many of them were eager to play.

At first Mr Scrivens would spend long periods of his allotted time at the school just playing and it was the kind of music that they were not accustomed to, intended for more educated ears than those of the children of farm labourers who were used to fiddle tunes and country songs. But this was the music that Lady Mountfield was insistent that the children should play –

Bach and Beethoven, she was convinced, would one day flow from their rough, poorly-educated hands. Mr Scrivens did not know rightly what he thought of this, it conflicted with his view of the lower classes and he was somewhat scornful of his employer's grand plan, but it paid well, in fact it paid very well indeed and who was he to question the power of pounds, shillings and pence.

He was under no illusion that his task would be an easy one, seated in front of three dozen, grubby upturned faces, demonstrating his skill for the fourth Monday in succession. He had not let a single one of them place their soiled fingers on the keys – yet – but he knew this would have to change very soon if he were to keep this lucrative employ. For the last three Mondays he made the children tap out a scale on their desks, chanting the notes aloud in chorus, but today he faced the onerous duty of finding out whether any of them had even the remotest aptitude for the instrument.

Once he had finished playing, he turned to Miss Adam and, as had previously been arranged and it being a fine day, she instructed the children to stand up and go out into the yard. Lessons would take place outside that day, while inside, one by one, the entire class would troop in to be tested.

The first chosen was John Graham's son, Mathew, a confident boy of ten years old, who marched quickly back into the school room, only to appear moments later in a state of confusion and trying but failing to hold back his tears. Mr Scrivens had simply asked the boy to show him his hands, which he had done obediently, the upturned palms outstretched in front of him. What he had not been prepared for was the crack of the ruler as it came down on first his left and then his right palm. "How dare you come in here with your hands in that state boy," he had raged at pour Mathew Graham. "Have you so little respect for the great privilege that Lady Mountfield is offering you? Now go and scrub your hands clean this instant, and if you are very lucky, I will see you again at the end of the day." And with those words he had been dismissed.

Miss Adam could barely contain her indignation at Mr Scriven's treatment of poor Mathew Graham, for what gave this man the right to discipline a pupil in her schoolroom? No sooner had this angry thought flashed across her mind, than the answer to her unvoiced question followed closely on its heels. Of course, she knew only too well what gave him the right. This man had the full weight of the school's benefactress behind him – and how could she gainsay his authority with Esther Mountfield's charity applauding his every step? Eliza Adam was young to the post, being only twenty-two years old herself, and perhaps, the piano master had already sensed her inexperience and had already formed a low opinion of her. Perhaps he had gone further and truly considered her to be only slightly more educated than these country children whom she was charged to teach.

But Eliza Adam was a determined young woman and now was not the time to be plagued by self-doubt and so she simply pushed those thoughts from her mind. After all, had she not come so far already on her young life's journey? Despite all the obstacles that had been put in her way, she had earned her place as the teacher in this little parish, and she would not now be put down by the first man who came along and challenged her position simply because he was a man.

Every nerve in her body jangled with indignation against the man's arrogance and prejudice and she determined that no more of her class would suffer the same treatment at the hands of this haughty man. She instructed her charges to line up at the outside tap and to scrub their hands clean and for the older ones to assist the younger ones in this task. Then she turned on her heel and walked briskly back into the schoolroom.

With dignity, though she found it difficult to disguise the trembling in her voice, she informed Mr Scrivens he would have to wait for the next pupil in order that they could all wash their hands. "This is a village school Mr Scrivens, set up for the express purpose of educating the sons and daughters of farmhands and labourers. I would have thought that as an educated man, you would have the wit to realise that these children are not the sons and daughters of gentlefolk, with armies of staff to pamper and coddle them and to wash their hands in lavender water! In future if you have a difficulty with any of my pupils, I would be grateful if you would refer your concerns to me!" She waited for the man to protest, but amazingly, slowly his stern, starched expression changed and she thought she could nearly discern the merest trace of a smile form on his lips.

If the truth be told, the piano master had not taken the trouble to look at Miss Adam until that very moment, despite this being the fourth visit he had made to the school. Could it be that he had indeed formed a completely wrong impression of the school mistress, having dismissed her simply as no more than a timid slip of a girl herself? And moreover, one who could surely have no real skill as a teacher, being only required in such a place as this to teach the most rudimentary of lessons to these poor ignorant souls. And yet here she was standing before him, indignant and passionate at his casual treatment of one of her urchins, her expression determined and her command of the English language quite simply astonishing to his previously prejudiced ears. Perhaps after all there would be more to draw him to this little Bedfordshire village each week, than simply the generous stipend paid to him by Lady Mountfield. Mr Scrivens continued to smile and very quickly began to build bridges with the young school mistress.

"My dear Miss Adam, I am justly brought to book, please accept my apologies. I would be most grateful if you would put this poor music scholar's over-zealousness down to a genuine love of his craft. Please be assured I will explain this to the boy when he comes before me again. Do pray, what was the child's name?"

"Mathew Graham," she responded simply, surprised and curiously delighted, though she knew not why, at the softening of the implacable music master.

"I am a strict teacher, Miss Adam, but as you so rightly pointed out, these are perhaps not the sort of children that I am used to. Let us say that I have learnt something today as well as your charges, and I would be grateful if we could put this matter behind us and make a fresh start."

"Of course, Mr Scrivens, let us do exactly that. I will send the next child in to you straight away." And she turned on her heel again, with the sweet taste of victory thrilling through her. Perhaps after all she had been too quick to judge the piano master.

All that morning the rest of the class had half an ear to the sounds emanating from the school room, and none of them were particularly cheerful – a mixture of clearly wrongly played notes, punctuated by Mr Scriven's increasingly exasperated interjections of 'No! No!' and at one point; 'For heaven's sake child you are playing the pianoforte not milking a cow!' Miss Adam sighed to herself; clearly, he was as strict a teacher as he had boasted.

At 12.00 o'clock Miss Adam rang the school bell for the lunch time interval, and dismissed the class, but she made sure to remind the children who had not yet been tested by Mr Scrivens to wash their hands twice before returning to school for the afternoon session. She turned and went back inside only to find Mr Scrivens in a far better mood than she had anticipated, in fact he seemed almost cheerful. "Well Miss Adam, I can't say that this morning has produced many promising candidates, but perhaps the afternoon will go better, do you not think?"

"Oh, I do hope so, Mr Scrivens, for Lady Mountfield will be so disappointed if there is not one amongst my charges who is eager to learn, for she has her heart set upon it," replied the school mistress.

"My dear young woman, I can assure you

your pupils are, how shall I put it, surprisingly enthusiastic to learn, but sadly it is their musical ears that I find fault with. As you so courteously reminded me, they are the sons and daughters of simple folk, and many, let me put this as delicately as I can, for I do not wish to offend you again, many have a very basic approach when it comes to learning an instrument."

Eliza, this time was not offended, as he had tried to put it as gently as he could, just a little crestfallen.

Mr Scrivens continued over her reverie. "If only I could find one, just one who showed a little of the aptitude, dedication and intelligence necessary to master the instrument. And then there is the music that Lady Mountfield wishes them to learn. I fear it will be completely beyond them."

"Mr Scrivens, I would ask you please to be patient, if these children are as eager to learn as you say, you must just give them time. Might I dare say, Mr Scrivens, if you were just a little gentler with them, then you might see some better results."

"Miss Adam, I will not, cannot alter my teaching methods. If they truly wish to learn, then they must be prepared to work hard and know from the start that I will be strict. Is that understood?" However, seeing the downcast looks of the school mistress, he softened his last remark with the words; "Please Miss Adam, do not despair, I am sure that this afternoon will yield results, I will not lose heart and neither must you."

At 2.00 pm the children returned to school and again found that their lessons were to continue outside the classroom while Mr Scrivens conducted his tests inside. My sister Rose was to tell me later, how she had fretted almost to the point of tears, before she even entered the schoolroom, for she so dearly wanted to learn how to play and was dreadfully afraid that she would not be up to the task. But once inside she took a deep breath and determined to answer the piano master's tasks as best she could. He had nodded at her, and at times shown his displeasure with a hard look, but he had not, and she perceived this to be a good sign, he had not raised his voice.

Mathew Graham, with a sinking heart, was the last to be seen that day. It was as if the whole class held their breath whilst he was in there, and no-one was more relieved than Miss Adam when he reappeared some fifteen minutes later, holding his hands aloft and with a defiant grin on his face.

Not long afterwards Eliza Adam dismissed her charges for the day, explaining that she would need to discuss with Mr Scrivens the results of his tests.

My sister Rose was the first to be chosen, along with a genuinely surprised Mathew Graham and three other boys; Peter Wood, Bob Turner and Arthur Wilkinson who were all a little older than my sister. The only other girl to be chosen was eleven-year-old Emmy White, who on account of her being a little slow at her studies was shocked to tears to discover that she would receive the coveted tuition. But of them all, it was my sister who had caught the piano master's attention, not that she could play any better than the rest, but there was just the faintest glimmer of promise in the way that she approached her audition that had made her stand out. If he were a betting man, which he most certainly was not, Mr Scrivens would have betted on my sister to excel above the rest.

Perhaps there was something incongruous about the pleasure that those six children found in the simple act of learning to play, given that the world was shifting under all our feet with each step we took during those long years of war. Perhaps not. Every Monday morning for three years, Mr Scrivens came to the school to teach and the six chosen children, despite their humble upbringings, week after week made progress and my sister most of all, staying late after school each day in order to practice the more.

Those three years saw changes in Eliza Adam and her piano master too. There were just little things at first to our untrained eyes, the offering of a flower that Mr Scrivens had picked from the lane as he walked from the station one morning, the straightening of a frock, where little care was seen before, under the shadow of war their gentle courtship made us titter and smile and whisper behind our sticky hands.

The year came and went, 1914 came and went and still those six children practiced their scales in the little school room. December 1914 turned into January 1915 and as the year turned the youngest men of the village began to disappear from the lanes around Long Wendon, following their fathers and brothers to the front. Some were not seen again for many years, if at all. As the older boys in the school room grew into young men, their mothers became anxious and with good cause, for one by one they turned their faces towards the army and marched away.

In June 1916 Mr Scrivens made his final visit to our school. What use would a piano master be with a gun in his hand? But he could resist the call no longer, and just like all the rest, plough boys, doctors and sons of the landed gentry, the once-stern piano master felt compelled to go. On the steps of our little school that last day he left Eliza Adam with a hurriedly brushed away tear in her eye that every one of us children saw, but not a one of us dared breathe a word on.

The following week my sister was given notice that she should report to Grange Park twice a week after school, and that she was to receive tuition from Lady Mountfield herself until Mr Scrivens should return from the army. Moreover, Rose was to take on the instruction of the younger children as best she could, and teach them the rudiments of playing. And so it was that at six years old I finally got my wish just as my sister had promised I would, I learned how to play the magical box, and it was my sister Rose who taught me how.

CHAPTER 6

LETTERS FROM KENNY HOUSE

William

Edward Mountfield was a Lieutenant in the 2nd Battalion of the Bedfordshire's. It was said of him that he was a fair man, decent and thoughtful to the men under his command, but they also said that you might as well have set a fish loose to swim in the woods than expect a man like Mountfield to find his place in the arena of war. He followed orders to the letter, but was imbued with an indecisive heart that rendered his military career average at best. Throughout the two long years that he served, there was not one mention of Lieutenant Edward Mountfield in dispatches.

Perhaps it was a mercy when a mortar attack left him unfit for further duties. But a mercy that had a sting in its tail, a mercy that left Edward Mountfield the man, a shadow of the fresh-faced Lieutenant who had signed up so eagerly in 1914. War changes people and Edward Mountfield was no exception, he left the army with a cane to help him stand and an inescapable belief that his luck to be alive and out of the fight had not been deserved.

August 12, 1916, Kenny House

Dear Mama,

Thank you for your parcel, it reached me in good order and the contents are enough to keep my spirits buoyant, though I have nothing truly to complain of. The nurses are all kindness and my return to health is due in most part to their diligent care of me.

Regarding your visit, I would advise a delay of a week or two, for even the shortest stay of a visitor is tiring to me. It would be better if you were able to wait until my physical recovery matches the rallying of my spirits. Please put your mind at rest as to my treatment, for I can assure you that I am not forgotten. Indeed, we at Kenny are not neglected, as the gentlewomen of Kingston upon Thames visit us regularly and without fail.

I will write again soon.

Your loving son,
Edward

August 19, 1916, Grange Park

My dearest Edward,

I do so wish that you would let me visit at the earliest convenience. It is not right to keep your Mama away like this. I have been so fearful for you, ever since I received the news, and it is a little cruel of you to keep me so at arm's length. I am stronger than you think dearest, and if I have not heard from you within a week saying that you are expecting me, then I shall come straight to Kenny House, and oust those usurping ladies from Kingston who administer to you in my rightful place.

My dear son, there is another pressing matter that you must deal with and at once before the dear young lady in question is distressed any further. You must write to Julia for I fear she will quite wear me out with her persistence. I know she has written to you several times, for she has told me so, but you must with all speed send her a reply.

I am determined that I shall see you very soon.

Your loving Mama

August 27, 1916, Kenny House

Dear Father,

I hope the shock of Mother seeing me in this

condition was not too alarming for her. I did try to dissuade her from coming until I was better prepared to receive her as a visitor. It must have been very upsetting, and you must reassure her that I am decidedly better than I must have appeared to her maternal eye.

Indeed, I am recovering well from my injuries and the doctors are certain that in a month or two I shall be fit enough to travel home to Grange Park. I shall certainly be in time for poor Peter's memorial and will of course say something at the service should it meet with your approval.

I know your loss is deeply felt and I only wish that you had let me intercede with Arthur before the damned fool enlisted. I have written to Colonel McWilliam and asked him to have a care of the boy and urged him to prevent the lad from doing anything damned foolhardy.

Regarding Mother, I hope you don't mind me suggesting that you ask Aunt Eleanor to stay, for I believe her disposition and practicality would prove a tonic to the household at this time.

Sincerely,
Edward

September 4, 1916, Grange Park

Edward,

Regarding Eleanor, I will not countenance that woman in my house. Your Mother is coping as best she can and she does not need Aunt Eleanor as a wet-nurse to her affairs. I have no doubt that she will bear this tragedy in time with the correct dignity as we all must. Let us say no more on the subject but look forward to your arrival at home.

Sincerely,
Your Father

September 12, 1916, Grange Park

Dear Edward

I have asked the servants to arrange rooms for you on the ground floor. I hope this will suit you. It is all so very difficult trying to organise things in your absence, not knowing what will be sufficient to your needs and with the household all a stir at the prospect of seeing you home at last.

It is harvest time, and there are so many children about in the fields just now, on account of their fathers being at the front. Sometimes I cannot look out of the lounge windows without seeing the provoking sight of dozens of them, as if the field were a common playground. But I should not complain, it is just that I cannot see how this army of urchins can ever bring in the harvest. But alas, these are the times we live in, and I must make sacrifices.

Julia has visited many times and complains that you have been neglectful. Please, please write to her with all speed. It is quite un-gentlemanly of you to treat her in this way. As your fiancée she expects at the bare minimum to be kept informed of your progress.

I will keep this letter very brief, as there is so much to do and the house is in an uproar.

Your loving Mama

CHAPTER 7

HOMECOMING

William

The memorial service for Sir Peter Mountfield's second son was a curiosity to me. It was exactly two years to the day since that young man had left for the fields of France that his remains and effects were shipped home to England. Except that I speak metaphorically of course, for there were no physical remains to ship. In the chaos of the Great War, returning a body to its loved ones was rarely possible and the young officer had been buried near to where he had died.

I was six years old and quite simply bowled away by the majesty and pomp and black satin finery that crammed into the little church at Long Wendon. It was as a matter of course accepted that the whole village would turn out to pay their respects to the landowner's fallen son, and as dutiful tenants our mothers scrubbed our faces clean, pressed our shirts and polished our shoes so we were to a child as clean, pressed, polished and scrubbed as we had never been before.

It was also the week of Edward's return to Grange Park, and he cut a frail figure as he stood at the altar and read the eulogy to his brother. There was an excitement to the whole occasion that I marvelled at, not yet touched by the sadness of comprehension that grows out of the wisdom of age, I was merely a bystander to the Mountfield family's grief and I drank it all in like a visitor to another world. With the hindsight of years, I should be ashamed of the avid curiosity that possessed me that day in a place where only sadness should have borne witness, but in truth I cannot be blamed for I was only a boy of six.

My sister Rose shed tears for her benefactress's dead son, but even my sister could not rightly say why she had cried, only that it seemed fitting that she should. As we filed out of the church, Lady Mountfield spoke in turn to our mothers and the old men of the village thanking them for their attendance. They mumbled humble words of condolence in return. But my most vivid memory of the day was of the woman standing between Lady Mountfield and her eldest son; why this impressed upon my memory so keenly I cannot say, perhaps only because it was so unexpected. As we children filed out at our mothers' sides this smartly dressed young woman pressed a penny into each of our hands. This gift of alms to the poor was exceedingly welcome to us and exceedingly strange all at the same time, coming as it did at a time of great family loss.

The smart lady wore a flattering black taffeta and satin dress, she was slim of build and of average height. Her hair was auburn and swept up to the back of her head on which was perched a neat small hat trimmed with a few purple flowers. She was not exactly pretty, but she was also not a plain girl having two liquid brown eyes and pale, perfect skin. But it was the scent that she wore that caught my attention as she pressed the coin into my hand with her gloved fingers, the scent of rose petals and crushed lavender, that and the sweet small smile and the kind warm eyes that assured me that she was sincere, I knew at once that here was a kind and loving soul. Edward Mountfield stood by her side, leaning awkwardly on his cane. His smartly dressed companion was Julia Asgarth.

"Hey Billy," whispered John in my ear, "Meet me by the school and we'll go climbing for conkers."

"Not in those clothes John Grant or your mother'll have something to say! Now run along and change the pair of you and mind you're back by teatime Will Baxter! And walk!" my mother hurriedly whispered as we were about to run full pelt away from the church gate.

As John and I were walking, it seemed like

snails, away from the funeral party I saw Esther Mountfield approaching my mother and Rose.

"Lily, would you send Rose up to the house tomorrow afternoon. I would like her to play for me, she's doing so well you should be proud of her."

"Yes, thank you, ma'am. That I am, right proud of her. I'll see she's there tomorrow in good time."

Lady Mountfield's gaze had drifted towards the comic sight of John and I trying to give the impression of a slow and dignified pace while walking really, really fast as we made our escape and ending up looking like a pair of circus clowns instead. We felt her eyes on us and slowed right down again, but clearly the great lady was not offended as she sighed. "Your youngest boy is growing again I see Lily. Send him up to the house with his sister and I'll get Cook to find him something to eat, he looks half-starved." And with that she turned on her heel and went back to the waiting party of gentry folk.

I sensed Rose appraising me critically her eyes boring into my back and I heard her saying to my mother. "Billy does look a bit like a scarecrow Mum, he's gone that skinny lately like a hazel stick!"

My mother smiled and hugged my sister. "He's just growing love, like boys do." If she was affronted by Lady Esther's assumption that she could barely feed her children, she didn't show it, but then who could gainsay the mistress of the big house on such an occasion as this. My mother knew full well that Esther Mountfield meant no slight to her, but she also knew that being poor sometimes gave the wealthy a licence to be thoughtless in their acts of charity.

CHAPTER 8

GRANGE PARK

William

It was Saturday afternoon and normally at this time I would be racing with my friend John Grant through the fields, chasing rabbits, butterflies, crows, scrumping apples, falling out of trees, scraping my shins and knees and elbows on rocks and stones and sliding on grass. But not today. Today I had to accompany my sister Rose to the big house and the only reason that I had not dug in my heels and protested most fiercely about the injustice of my situation was due to the prospect of filling my skinny body with food scraps from the cook's kitchen. I was after all six years old, growing fast and permanently hungry – so hungry that at times my joints would ache and my belly would crease up with stinging pains. But I was still not entirely happy with my lot.

"Why do I have to go? I want to play with John."

"You'll do as you're told Will and do it with a good grace my boy. What would your father say if he were here to see you make such a fuss?"

my mother reprimanded. Sullenly I accepted my sister Rose's outstretched hand, and feeling very overdressed, not to say hot and uncomfortable in my Sunday best clothes for the second day in a row, I let her lead me out of the front door, along the lane that led out of the village and along the top road that led to the start of a long tree-lined avenue. It was September time and the sun spiked through the poplars that ran the length of the drive and by the end of it my little legs felt that it must have been at least a hundred miles long.

I was about to march up to the front door when Rose yanked me by the arm and pulled me in a contrary direction. My gaze remained sideways as she ushered me along, for I had not seen in all my days such a house as this with its huge bronze-plated door, high arches and carvings ornately surrounding its most impressive entrance way. To finish the effect a twisted wisteria overarched and framed the doorway with a wash of pale violet petals that were now falling like confetti onto the swept and tended driveway.

"How many families live here?" I asked my mouth agape.

"Just one, silly," replied my sister, with a gentle laugh.

"They must be very, very rich," I said.

"Course they are Billy, that's why they've got titles. You have to be rich to have titles in front of your name."

"What are titles?" I asked.

"You know Billy, think! They're not called Mr and Mrs like ordinary folks, they're called Sir Peter and Lady Mountfield, that's what titles is."

"When I grow up, I want to live in a castle and have titles!" I said.

At this my sister laughed out loud; "Course you will Billy, you'll have any title you want, even King if you like, what about that?"

"Oh Rose, do you really think so? You're not making fun of me."

She put her arm around my shoulder and looked at me with a glittering smile; "I'd never make fun of you, you're my brother, and if you want to be King Billy of England, King Billy you'll be! Come on, let's find Mrs Stewart, she's the cook and she's real nice, but just mind you say please and thank you like Mum taught us. Oh, yes and smile your best smile Billy, that way she'll be sure to take to you."

And with that we half skipped, half ran round the side of the house to the back entrance, which wasn't half so grand.

Rose, as bold as brass walked right in and as we entered the kitchen, still holding tight to my hand, pulled me swiftly behind her as she wove round the small army of kitchen staff who were returning with empty dishes and pots and plates from the dining room and the family's luncheon. She stopped in front of a formidable looking woman, all swaddled in long white skirts, a cap on her head and a not so clean apron which she now removed. She was tall and plump and her face was flushed but it was not an unpleasant face for all that. She had mouse coloured hair and cornflower blue eyes and when she set them on my sister, she did not seem displeased to see her.

"So, it's you is it, Rose Baxter?" she said with a commanding voice.

"Yes Mrs Stewart, Lady Mountfield sent for me, and she said to bring Billy too."

Mrs Stewart turned to look at me, and without thinking, for I had never met a 'cook' before and therefore imagined her to be just as grand as Sir Peter and Lady Esther having the title of 'cook', that I put one arm behind my back and wrapped the other round my waist and bowed as low as I could. "I'm pleased to meet you, Mrs Stewart." I said and then, remembering what Rose had told me, I added my best smile onto the end of my bow.

Mrs Stewart could not contain her laughter. She reached out and ruffled my hair as if she had known me all her life. "Well bless my soul," she said "he thinks I'm a lady! Child you don't have to bow to me, I am the cook, but I am very pleased to meet you too Billy. Now, you look like you could eat a meal or three young man, so let's see what we can find you."

My cheeks burned red with confusion as I was ushered to the end of a long wooden kitchen table and took my place beside my sister who by this time was chatting merrily away to her neighbour, a sallow-faced girl whom I supposed to be four or five years older than Rose herself. We feasted with the rest of the servants in the kitchen, for it was their custom to eat together after the family had been served, and so we were joined by nearly a dozen household staff and a further twenty or so who worked on the estate and in the grounds.

There was a great clattering and scraping of plates and cutlery and the atmosphere was all hum and bustle. I saw eyes flash across the table as serving girls flirted with the few men and boys who were left to work on the estate. I saw sad looking faces and merry ones too, faces with plenty of care in them, and those with none in the world, faces just happy to be in the here and now, with thoughts not drifting beyond that here and now or turned outwards to thinking of loved ones across the sea. There was much talk, some earnestly discussing the progress of the war, some light-hearted banter and play, and as I watched and ate my fill of the plate put in front of me, I thought what a good place this would be to live and to work when I was grown.

"He don't say much, do he?" I heard Mrs Stewart speaking to Rose.

"No, Mrs Stewart he likes to watch, always has, he's funny like that."

"You'd best finish up now, Rose and get along to the morning room, I expect Lady Mountfield'll be ready for you now. And take Billy with you, I'm sure he'd like to see that fine room, so long as he's quiet mind."

"I'll be as quiet as mice, I swear" I piped in earnestly.

"Just one mouse will do child, run along now the both of you."

Rose took me by the hand again and led me out of the kitchen by a different door to the one we had come in by.

We stopped in a small side room off the long corridor, being still in the servant's part of the house, and Rose hoisted me aloft until I sat on a wooden draining board next to a tap and trough-shaped basin. Slowly she pumped the handle and water came gushing out. I nearly fell off my perch open-mouthed. Rose laughed out loud. "Haven't you seen a tap before!" she teased making her eyes big and round with mock astonishment.

"Course I have," I protested, "but this one's inside!"

"Course it is, Billy, where should it be?" And she continued laughing while she washed her face and hands and mine too, though I had been scrubbed clean by Mother before I had set out, so there was really no need.

"You never told me they was so grand that they have an inside tap?"

"They have lots of things Billy, you'd be amazed, lots of things I bet you won't even know the names of!" And with that she pulled me off the drainer and took my hand once again. She only stopped laughing once we had gone some distance, past the servants' staircase and through to the main part of the house. As we entered the family's rooms, I really did think I was entering a palace.

CHAPTER 9

EDWARD MOUNTFIELD

Edward

"Damn it, Esther, I will not tolerate this in my own house. Not today! I will not listen to your prized guttersnipe tapping out common tunes on the pianoforte, no matter how many times you tell me that it will lift my spirits. The girl is barely more than a beggar and your indulgence of her will only make her impertinent. I will be in the drawing room with any civilized company that wish to join me!"

And with that my father slammed out of the room, striding forcefully away from my mother and the rest of the luncheon party. The Reverend and Mrs Hawkins, though clearly straightened as to which way to turn and fearing they would offend one or the other of my parents whatever they did, reluctantly left the room. They were followed by Arthur, who was home on leave fortuitously, having completed his basic training, but who in three days' time would leave for the front with the rest of his regiment.

He raised his eyes briefly heavenward with a nonchalant grin, and then proceeded to saunter out of the room. As he was leaving, a young girl of about nine or ten years old was entering, her eyes taking in the scene of hostility that my father had just exited from.

Arthur wagged a finger at the child, who was accompanied by a very thin boy who was a few years younger than the girl and looked scared out of his wits. "My, my, pretty Rose, what a hornet's nest you've stirred up child by your merest presence." And with that he pinched the girl's cheek and left the room, pointedly closing the door behind him.

"Why does he act so vilely? Now I have a blinding headache and will have to go and lie down! He does not take proper account of the good and charitable work that I do."

"Excuse me ma'am," interrupted the object of my mother's charity. "Shall we go home now?"

"Good gracious no, are you simple girl? You have only just got here. You will do as I would have you do and practice." Turning to Julia she continued; "Be a dear and listen to Rose would you, for I must surely lie down before my head splits in two."

She turned to go as I began to protest, "Mother, Julia is not part of the staff. Perhaps Mrs Downley will oblige?" I continued, naming our housekeeper as a more appropriate choice than my fiancée.

"Edward, Lady Esther, please I really don't mind. I would like to hear the child play." And before I could utter another word my mother swept out of the room with a gesture that precisely matched my father's of a few moments earlier.

I was trapped by my fiancée's willing acquiescence to my mother's whim and felt my irritation rising even before the child spoke.

"Sir, we had much better go home." She held her brother's hand tightly to make herself bold. "I will say to Lady Mountfield that I stayed and practised right hard when she asks, Sir. I promise I will."

She looked me fiercely in the eye, her two dark pupils unafraid of this unexpected encounter with her benefactress' son and the odd predicament in which she had been left. It was a look of such unexpected assuredness, a gaze that almost fooled me into agreeing to her proposed deception.

"Sit down child and do as my mother has bidden." I spoke firmly but not unkindly, for it was not after all the fault of the child.

I do not know what she saw in my disposition or in my eyes, perhaps I had not hidden my annoyance deep enough but for a moment and to my great astonishment I thought that she would gainsay me. She stood rooted to the spot, not moving a muscle. Her brother by this time was positively trembling beside her.

"Your mother is unwell Sir, and, and…"

But this time her courage failed her. I had my acquiescence and so softened my voice, all the while musing what it was about this village girl that so intrigued me. I ended the sentence that the child had begun; "… and you thought to spare Julia and myself the trouble, is that it?"

She looked down and whispered her reply, "Yes Sir."

"Well, then, if that is truly what you meant, we shall say no more about it. You should not disappoint my mother, however, so it appears for the time being you must stay."

Again, she whispered; "Yes sir," her boldness quite vanished and I found myself unexpectedly disappointed by her sudden lack of spirit. Had she feared me? Was I such a callow specimen that I could scare children with my poorly concealed bad humours? As if I could, in my straightened condition cause any genuine harm to the girl, so firmly was my hand now fixed to my cane that was itself the very prop by which I stood. It could have no other use.

Julia smiled at me, her eyes full of unspoken approval as she took the boy gently by the hand

and walked him to the open verandah doors. What did she see when she now laid eyes on my broken and unnatural frame; it was certainly not the likeness I saw in my shaving mirror each morning. But would I, in truth, rather have her pity than her devotion. I could not yet say.

I watched her closely as she sat the boy down on the verandah step and began to speak to him gently, calmly, all the while putting him at his ease, as if... as if she had been acquainted with him her whole life – this ragged half-starved soul. As it so often had before, but even more so now since my return from France, her gentleness unmanned me. Her kindness left me wretched and unequal. Was this tenderness that she now showed for the boy, the same tenderness that I so recoiled from when she looked on me? How would I find a way to send her from me?

I forced my gaze back to Rose, who by this time had seated herself at the piano. Her clothes were neat but worn and in places well darned or patched. Her hair was pulled back from her face and snaked down her back in a long plait. She looked completely out of place in the finery of my parents' drawing room, stiff backed and not quite humbled by my rebuke. What was my mother thinking to bring her into our home? For once I was of a mind to agree with my father.

"What are you waiting for, girl?" I said sharply, too sharply.

"What should I play Sir?" she whispered, her eyes peering out from under dark lashes.

I once again caged my temper. "Just play what you would normally play if my mother were here." And with that I eased myself down into the large armchair that was adjacent to the piano, the better to observe the girl.

She tilted her head in acknowledgement, her lips pursed with assent, and started to run her long fingers up and down the keys with a practised ease. She started with a series of scales and arpeggios, neatly and perfectly performed while I appraised her more keenly than when she had first entered the room.

She was, when all was said and done, quite the most beautiful child I had ever laid eyes on, and for this alone I could see why my mother had acquired her. She was slight of build, with milk-white skin, a blush of pink in her cheek, black straight hair that shone with just a hint of red running through it and then there were those eyes. Round, large, like two black pools of night staring back at me. I supposed that they could not really be black, but were certainly the darkest brown, like soft doe's eyes that pierced you through. I was quite taken aback by her physical presence, as if she were some kind of faery child – a ragged angel sitting amongst all the finery of my parents' furniture and my mother's pretty china and glass ornaments, but this living waif was by far the prettiest of them all. Sitting at the stool in her muted, drab clothes, her unexpected grace and poise confounded me for here was beauty where it had no place to be.

I was still less prepared for the girl's undoubted talent as she began to play. I had not expected to hear such music brought to life under her hands, nor see the skill with which her bitten fingers traced their patterns across the notes, nor guessed at the way her child's body swayed in complete accord with the composer's sure intention. How could I? This was the daughter of a labourer turned soldier, with worn thread-bare shoes and patched Sunday clothes.

She played the long piece, I know not what it was, until its end. It was not a faultless rendition, with here and there a wrong note, a slipped finger, but the piece was not the country air my father had predicted but a refined and gentle composition, which demanded a great deal of the player. Whenever she had faltered, which was not often, she had corrected her mistake, and the overall impression that she made was quite extraordinary. Too soon the music finished, but I was curiously thirsty for more. "How long have you been playing girl?" I asked.

"Three years, Sir."

"You show much skill for such a short time, Rose. Now, would you play this piece again if my mother were here?"

"Yes Sir, and there is another piece too. I usually play for about an hour."

"Then continue with your practice."

I forced my attention back to Julia and the boy while Rose resumed her study. My fiancée had got his rapt attention as she turned the pages of a pictorial nature book for his pleasure showing him drawings of exotic creatures of the world and filling his head with facts and stories. I closed my eyes, listening to the truly uncommon skill of the wretched girl.

CHAPTER 10

JULIA ASGARTH

William

I heard raised voices as we went further into the occupied part of the house and Rose slowed our progress, hanging back as a clearly irate Lord Mountfield burst out of the room in front of us, slamming the door, followed a few minutes later by the Reverend Hawkins and a clearly flustered Mrs Hawkins. The Reverend acknowledged the sight of Rose and myself with a nervous, but encouraging smile, but then followed swiftly after the master of the house hurriedly drawing his wife behind him.

By this time Rose had her hand on the doorknob, but before she could open it, someone else came through the door. Arthur, the youngest son, halted, stepped back and made a grand gesture of holding the door for us, and Rose not hesitating for an instant walked straight through it, pulling me behind her. He spoke a few words to my sister to tease her, and then casually left, and I could clearly see the colour beginning to rise in my sister's cheek.

As soon as we entered the room, Lady Mountfield made her excuses to leave, which left only myself and Rose, the eldest son Edward Mountfield and the kind-hearted lady whom I had seen the day before at the funeral – Julia Asgarth.

I don't know what possessed my sister, for though she was fearless I did not know her foolhardy, for the next thing I knew she had proposed to Edward Mountfield that he collude with her in a bare-faced lie to his mother.

"I will say to Lady Mountfield that I stayed and practised right hard …" The words were out before she could stop herself.

Fear of what would come prickled up my spine and I felt my cheeks heat with blood and I'm sure to any observer my eyes must have widened with pure dread. But for a moment, just for a moment, I thought the master's son would agree and send us on our way. But that moment passed too quickly after all and then I began to fear that my sister was for it as I saw his hand flex on the handle of the cane he leaned on and truly I thought he would hurt her. I held my breath and closed my eyes.

Mercifully my fears came to nought for the young master for some inexplicable reason made his own excuse for my sister's bold mistake.

It all passed in a few seconds of time, but to

me that first exchange between my sister and Edward Mountfield seemed to last an eternity.

Looking back, with the eyes of years behind me, I now realise that for us all there are a handful of moments in childhood that inform and shape the adults we are to become. It was in that moment, though I knew it not at the time, that I first saw a levelling of the gulf that lay between us, a beat in time where there was no separation due to wealth or class, just a fleeting breath where my sister and the master's son looked each other in the eye and there was no distinction between maid and master and furthermore to my utter confusion it was the master not the maid who reached his hand out across the divide. A few words only and then the moment was passed, a few words only that would set the course for all that followed between my sister and Edward Mountfield, a few words that would intertwine their different worlds for better and worse. But I could not see it then, the years had not yet formed me. It is only with the surety of hindsight, right now, on this day and at this time, that that brief memory becomes as clear and sound to me as a ringing bell.

For the rest of that afternoon, I had the very great privilege, as I considered it then, of being in the exclusive company of Julia Asgarth. She was a lovely, sweet natured young woman, who showed me so much care and attention that afternoon that it was possible to forget myself, to forget that she was a fine lady and I was a child of the fields. We sat on the steps of the veranda, the windows flung wide open to the lawn and garden beyond and the smell of roses and honeysuckle wafting in, so at times it was difficult to discern where the scent of the flowers ended and the sweet scent of my companion's kindness began.

She wore a long, beige dress of finely woven cloth, with a gold, latticed belt around her waist that completed the fashionable look. Understated, but elegant, and as I was to know more of the lady, this was to become my enduring memory of her. She sat slightly sideways on the step, her legs folded to the left and the toe-points of the court shoes she wore resting lightly on the patio flagstones, for we sat half in and half out of the room. Laid out on the ground before us, was a large book which held beautiful, bold pictures of God's animal kingdom and with delight and patience she spent the afternoon filling my head with facts, descriptions and stories as she turned page after page to reveal colourful creature after colourful creature. So captivated was I by her charms that I cannot remember uttering a single word that whole afternoon. At that time, she would have taken my muteness for the shyness it was, though that condition was to become my reality within the space of a year.

It seemed so improbable to me at six years old that this lovely, warm human being was to become the wife of Edward Mountfield. I, of course, had not been old enough to know anything about the man before he went to war, although there were many in the village who were quick to defend this match, having known the master's son of old. But as the warming sun beat down, sitting on the stone steps with Julia Asgarth I could not reconcile my instinctive dislike for the man with my very distinctive like for his fiancée. Every pore of his body seemed to exude a meanness of spirit, whether real or imagined to my child's eye and as I stared at his stern, humourless face I could not picture them in a happy, contented future. If truth be told, I was a little afraid of him, of his stiff-backed stance and his physical appearance. He wore a black patch over his eye to mask his injury and there was a white, thin, scar that came from behind that patch and continued down the length of his cheek. His was truly the portrait of childhood horrors. You could still see that he had once been a handsome man, but now it was as if there was something lacking in his comportment, as if at times he were simply acting the part of the landowner's son and heir. I could not say for why, but still less did I like the way he stared so intently at my sister, as if studying her. How could she not feel the coldness of his eyes, the disdainful angle of his gaze upon her back as she practiced her scales and pieces?

CHAPTER 11

CHANGE

William

As the year turned from 1916 to 1917 my mother received news of my father's death. She bore the loss with resignation, weeping silently when she thought no-one would observe her, for why should she amongst the tens of thousands who suffered similar tragedies be spared her portion in the misery of this great war? Rose took the news very hard and often I would see her wiping fresh tears from her permanently swollen face. My mother would scold her now and then, urging her to take control of herself for there was no sense crying over what could not be changed. And I? I was like a witness to my family's grief, not able to feel the hurt myself and so I held my tongue. I was only four when I had last seen my father and the memory of him had all but faded from sight. Perhaps I had been too young when he had gone away, I don't know, but I know I felt a deep-seated, some would say irrational, guilt at not being able to join my mother and sister in their grieving.

As I approached my seventh birthday, I was told that I was to consider myself to be the man of the house 'til the day my brother Tom should return from the front. I tried to keep my lip from trembling as my mother mouthed the words – I suppose she thought it a way to bolster and comfort her children, but even as she spoke, I knew that such a notion was ridiculous. This burden weighed me down with its proclamation of responsibility and I was left simply confused and frightened that I would not live up to this weighty expectation. I was the same child I had been the day before and the day before that, and would be for the many days, months and years to come. I tried to speak the words of comfort that were seemingly demanded of me, but the words came out all wrong. They were the words of a child, meaningless comforts and the more I tried to live up to the task, the less I seemed fit for it. As a consequence, I found myself saying less and less, and not long after the rumours began, I simply stopped speaking at all.

With no wage being sent from our father, our immediate future became precariously uncertain. A week after we had received word of his death, a servant was sent with a summons to my mother to come that very afternoon to Grange Park. My mother fully expected to receive notice to quit our cottage and so it was for this reason that she set out alone, full of trepidation as to where we should go and how she would feed and clothe us now that her husband was dead.

She was admitted by way of the servant's entrance but was very swiftly ushered through to the family's rooms and it was not the overseer who greeted her as she had anticipated, but Lady Mountfield herself. The whole affair was settled in under half an hour, by which time my mother had been given a position as a maid of all work, for which she was to receive a small stipend, but more importantly she was to retain the lease of the cottage. It was not exactly an act of charity, for my mother would work hard and long hours for her pay, but she herself believed that it must be due in large part to the great lady's partiality for my sister Rose. As a consequence, both Rose and I spent more and more time round and about Grange Park.

Spring arrived early to our hamlet in that year of nineteen seventeen, and to outward appearance there was little change from all the spring seasons that I had known before. The eruption of new life came as it had done every year, following on from the snow and ice of winter and the lean months of the new year.

Rabbits aplenty skittered across the fields, providing a welcome source of meat to the villagers, and crops began to press up through the soil. In our small community the green shoots of our own plantings began to show in every patch of ground around our homes and throughout the Spring and Summer months, before and after school we children would join our mothers, aunts, grandmothers and grandfathers out on the land, tending, nurturing, ushering the seedlings towards the Autumn gathering when all the fruits of our labour would come to harvest. But for the absence of men of fighting age out in the fields, very little of the outward show had changed from 1913 save one – hope. Hope of an early conclusion to the war had all but gone, the return of husbands, fathers and sweethearts from the army was a long way off and only spoken of in hushed whispers lest we should frighten it further hence into the future. Thus, though the semblance of our lives was as it had always been, in reality it had vanished forever – the war had simply blown it away.

After school, my sister Rose and I would walk up to the big house. On days like today, when the air was still and the heat of the sun warmed us right through to our bones, I would hang back, scuffing my shoes in the dirt, making clouds of dust rise up and sparkle back down to the ground again. Every day after school, Rose would practice the piano under the watchful eye of Lady Mountfield, while I had the freedom of the grounds to roam around in as I wished, whilst

I waited for our mother to finish her work. At around 6 or 7pm each evening, the three of us, would walk back down the long drive to our home, my mother weary, my sister humming the sweet music she had just played over in her head and I, as ever, famished despite having struck up a great friendship with Mrs Stewart and the contents of the Mountfield's pantry.

As long as I kept well out of sight of Sir Peter Mountfield and any guests the family had staying, I found that I could please myself where I went in the gardens of Grange Park, the whole estate was one vast playground to me. There were many things to engage the attention of a small boy left to his own devices, whether it was to tag along behind Mr Frances the head gardener, who never seemed to mind my company, or to seek out the ornamental pond that lay just beyond the formal lawn.

The pond was at the back of the house and was separated from view, being on a lower level and bordered by a thin box hedge that ran its length. I had to be on my guard for the drawing room was quite often occupied, and if I was spotted, I was sure to receive a clout from one of the servants. But I didn't even mind that so much for the pond held many wonders, and for me the fascination of it outweighed the risk of getting caught. It was stocked with ornamental fish of every colour and hue that seemed to lollop and roll rather than swim in its' shallow depths. When I was sure that no-one was about, by that I mean walking on the formal lawn, for I could not be seen from the drawing room itself, and then again barely from the lawn as long as I stooped, I liked to dip my feet in the cool water. I would slip off my socks and shoes and walk amongst the giant fish, feeling the pond-weed round my ankles, the better to get a sight of these amazing creatures.

On one such late summer evening I was sitting on the edge of the pond, dipping my toes in the water and listening to the soulful music that my sister was playing, for the verandah doors must have been flung wide and the music was wafting out. I was just about to step into the pond, when I heard raised voices above me, coming closer. Quickly I snatched up my shoes and socks and flung myself down beside the box hedge. Unless they came down the steps to the pond, they would not see me, and indeed I had no choice, for I could not run for then I would surely have been discovered. I pressed myself into the hedge, holding my breath. I recognised the voices, though I could not see their faces, as those of Edward Mountfield and Julia Asgarth.

CHAPTER 12

DISCUSSIONS

Edward

"I will not keep you to your promise, Julia. We have been over and over the reasons, now let that be an end to this discussion. You are simply not being reasonable to think we can continue on this course." I had finally plucked up the courage to end our engagement and instead of accepting the situation, albeit with a few tears, sighs and regrets as I assumed she would, here she was stating that she did not want our contract to end. It was simply nonsensical of her! What able-bodied young woman would not take this as her cue to bow out gracefully? Here I was absolving her of her promise, offering her back her chance of happiness and she was making a hysterical scene.

"On this course? We are talking about our marriage Edward," she countered. "I have not stopped loving you because you were injured fighting for your country. What sort of a girl do you think I would be if I had?"

"I am not doubting your feelings, Julia; but you are young, you will get over this, you will find someone else."

"Don't patronize me, Edward. Have your feelings altered towards me? Is that it?" She looked me squarely in the eye. "For if they have not; you are the one who is being unreasonable. If we had married before you had gone away, as we had planned, we would not even be having this conversation."

It was true that like many of our generation we had become engaged shortly before hostilities had broken out across Europe, though I was only twenty-two at the time which was considered to be a very young age for one of my class and social position to contemplate forming a lasting attachment. But events abroad had overtaken our plans, and so we had waited, thinking that the war would not last long. And Julia was right of course, if we had proceeded with haste, we would not now be having this discussion. "For better or worse I would have been your wife," she concluded.

"And by not marrying we have avoided the worst; can you not see that?" I gripped the handle of the cane, regaining control, for I did not want to raise my voice to her, for she was right about one thing, I did still love this woman. But what good was I to her now? I was weary for this confrontation to end. "Julia, please, I do not want your pity, you would be binding yourself to a half man."

She was taken aback, and I saw the pity I so feared in her eyes as she laid her small hand over my larger one, moving closer, insinuating her body close to mine, so close I could feel the heat of her breath. "You are the same man that I fell in love with Edward," she whispered, her eyes full of pain and I hated her for it.

I flinched at the touch of her perfect hand cupped over mine, the frustration and rage growing inside me like a poison that I could not fight. Instinctively I threw her hand off. "I cannot give you what you want. Our marriage would be a sham, I cannot give you children, think of that." I threw this last at her with every ounce of bitterness and self-loathing I could muster. "I do not want a nurse maid and that is all you would be!"

"Edward, don't do this." Her voice was shocked by my viciousness, and I am ashamed to say I liked the sensation that this aroused in me. "If we do not marry, then it will be through your doing and not mine. I swear, I do not pity you, I rather think that you pity yourself. I will not give up on you as easily as you seem to be able to give up on me." And with that she turned on her heel and walked straight across the lawn and into the house.

I rocked back on my uninjured leg. Damn the woman! The easiest and selfish thing to do would be to acquiesce. Could she still love me? And could I still love myself if I let her stay and follow through with this miserable union?

I looked outward across the pond, the far lawn, and further to the fields beyond, the sun still high in the cloudless blue sky of this long hot Summer. I could feel the dull pain that now and then would spike up the back of my leg, as if to remind me, lest I could forget, the uselessness of my damaged limb. It was as if the mere thought of it provoked an attack and as I stood there staring out across the lawn I felt a spasm course up to my spine. I winced with the pain of it. Was this how it was to be from now on?

I gripped the handle of my cane more firmly and turned to face the house once more, only to see my mother, her long skirts billowing about her marching straight towards me across the lawn. What now?

"Edward, there you are." It was a proclamation, and where the devil did she think I would be? "I have asked Julia to stay for the rest of the Summer. Her family are only too willing to spare her, and she has proved such a comfort to me these last few weeks and the dear young girl has of course consented immediately. There what do you think of that? She will no doubt be a great comfort to you too."

I stared at my mother coldly. "I wish you would stop interfering mother." My response was clipped.

"Nonsense, darling, I wouldn't dream of it," she breezed on, "But you really should set a date for the wedding, it would bring us all so much joy."

"There isn't going to be a wedding." I kept my palpable anger at bay, just.

"Of course, there is. That poor girl has stood by you day and night, it is your responsibility to do the right thing by her."

"Do the right thing? You are being perfectly idiotic Mother. Look at me! I'm a cripple – doing the right thing as you say, is what I'm trying to do by letting her go."

"Don't say that word Edward, you demean yourself by it. And I dare say there's no need for you to think about 'letting her go'. That sweet, sweet girl is in love with you and she simply wouldn't countenance you letting her go as you call it. How could you even think such a thing?"

"This is between Julia and I, Mother, and I would thank you to keep out of my affairs." The anger was growing inside me, the poison burning with every second she stood there with her idle chatter, as if she could stage manage my life with her platitudes. But of course, she would play her final card, as she always did when she sought me out to discuss Julia.

"Your own brother Peter will never know the happiness that you are able to discard so easily," she sobbed. "I simply don't understand you at all, my own son. If you persist in this arrant folly, in rejecting this poor, sweet, devoted girl while you wallow in self-pity…" She could not finish the sentence as the sobs were coming thick and fast now.

It was useless to continue the discussion. I knew very well the implication. Peter was dead and I was alive and should be grateful to God who had spared me a similar fate and grateful again for the love of this girl who would have me despite my frailty. My mother by this time had turned away and was sobbing into her handkerchief.

"I need to lie down; my head is beating so," she continued to cry." Go and tell the child to finish her practice and to return again tomorrow at the same time." And with that she walked swiftly away, too swiftly for a man with a cane to keep step with her.

Of course, damn it all, the child had been playing all the while, the soft music an incongruous accompaniment to our exchange. And for the second time I was dismissed to deal with my mother's latest act of charity – the wretched, pretty girl who played so well, and had not the right.

I was stifling in this environment, so sure was I in my conviction that I was pitied and despised by my family, by the servants and by my oh-so persistent fiancée. And then there was the girl – and I knew as I walked towards the drawing room that it was on that child that all my wrath and frustration would be vented this day. Just like the battering tidal storms that without pause will send the endless waters of the ocean to pound against the shore, there was not a thing I could do to hold back the rage.

CHAPTER 13

WATCHING AT THE WINDOW

William

I heard the dull tap of the young master's cane on the ground as he walked away. Hurriedly I pulled on my socks and tied my shoelaces. While his back was turned, I sprinted to the side of the box hedge and took a wide circle around the edge of the lawn. As he entered the drawing room from the garden, I pressed myself along the side of the house and crept almost to the point of the open verandah doors. I sat down on the steps to listen.

"Rose!" His voice was brittle, loaded with intent. "My mother commands that you finish your practice and return tomorrow at the same time."

My sister stopped playing, "Yes Sir," she replied.

"I did not tell you to stop," he sneered the words at her, clipped, forced, guttural. "Continue. I will listen."

Quietly I nudged closer along the outside wall of the house so that at last I could peer around the open doors to get a better view. Like a moth to the flame, I was instinctually drawn to the little scene as it unfolded in the drawing room, I could not say for why, neither could I look away.

The cold chill of foreboding had me clenched in a tight grip. The master's face was a portrait in ugliness, the thin mask of civility had utterly gone and in its place was nothing but a raw and wretched creature, full of self-loathing and disgust. His cold, cruel eyes were fixed intently on my sister as he struggled to control his visceral instincts.

Rose resumed her study. I could hear in the way that she played that she was unnerved for her playing was tentative. The music continued for a few moments, the master's son close behind my sister, stiffly watching – surely, she must feel his very breath on the back of her neck? Without warning I saw him slam the lid of the piano down over the keys. From this angle I could only see part of what transpired, for her hands were disguised from view by his body, but on hearing no sound from my sister I knew that she had snatched her fingers away in time.

The next moment I watched, hardly daring to breathe as Edward Mountfield pulled my sister roughly from the piano stool to stand before him, his voice betraying an anger and coldness of purpose that I had never heard before.

"My mother has given you this extraordinary opportunity and you squander it as if it were nothing." He spat the words at her. "Your playing was very poor indeed. Because my mother is not in the room to hear you practice, that does not mean you should not give your full attention to the task."

My sister's reply was not much above a whisper. "I'm sorry Sir, I did mean to play well."

"Do not lie to me, girl." I watched with a sickening sense of powerlessness not knowing what next would transpire. My breath was quite still while my heart beat fiercely in my small chest.

A heartbeat more and Edward Mountfield looked down along the length of his good arm, his cane now discarded. He looked to where he held my sister captive in his grip, the fingers of his hand digging into her pale flesh. He seemed to stutter, to halt, confusion washed over his features to be replaced in the next moment by a look of such sorrow and shame it was difficult to witness. It passed across his face and then was gone. Another heartbeat; he released her arm and she sank back down onto the stool. 'I'm sorry, so… so very…" he whispered. Without his cane he teetered like an unsteady foal. Rose was up on her feet again in an instant and quickly came to his aid, ushering him to his chair, quickly retrieving his cane where it had fallen, and pressing it firmly into his unsteady hand.

The eyes he cast on her must have been haunting to behold, broken. He stayed her movement, releasing his cane only for it to fall once again at his feet and gently ever so gently took her hand in his. My sister held his gaze.

"I have no right to ask this of you. I cannot… Forgive me, there are not words… I…" He could not force the words from his lips.

"Sir?"

"Play for me? I do not command you to do it, but I would very much like to hear you play." He released her fingers.

A beat, nothing more. "As you wish," she replied. A silence hung between them, as I waited for my sister to set her fingers once more on the keys and play. At last, the music came, sweet, haunting and this time unerring. It continued for quite some time, until I heard the young master's voice again, altered, calmed, defeated by my sister's skill. "Thank you, Rose. Go home child."

She ran straight out of the verandah doors and across the lawn. Not caring whether Edward Mountfield saw me or not, I raced after her as fast I could, only catching her once she had rounded the corner of the house and slowed to a walking pace. I caught up with her and flung my arms about her waist to hug her. I looked up into her face, then at her bare arm where I could clearly see the print of Edward Mountfield's fingers, angry and red where he had held her. I felt a tear roll down my face, then felt the trace of her hand as she wiped it away. "Hush Billy," she soothed, whipping back her hair defiantly but her eyes too had welled up with tears.

"I hate him," I said.

She looked at me quizzically for some time as if she were thinking all the while what she should say, how she could explain it to me, how best to soothe the rage that looked up at her from my wet, dark eyes. She spoke gently, softly, her voice no more than a whisper. "He wasn't angry at me, not really," she said, biting her lip nervously. She saw my puzzled expression. "Mum says he's angry at everyone and everything since he's come back from the war. But mostly he's angry at himself, that's what Mum says." But I did not care about him, not then. I could not find the smallest speck of sympathy that would excuse this random act of cruelty to my sister. All I felt was hate.

She pressed on with words that she had clearly learnt by rote, though the unexpected compassion in them was all hers. "He's a cripple Billy. He's been at the war and fought for his country and come back crippled. We should feel sorry for him, Billy. That's what Mum says." And all the while her silent tears splashed down the front of her dress.

Of course, I knew nothing of the remorse that Edward Mountfield felt as he watched Rose dash from the room, as he saw me break from the cover of my hiding place and scramble after her as fast as my legs would carry me. Not until years later did I learn how he had stared after us both until we had long disappeared from sight.

CHAPTER 14

RAGE

Edward

I listened without seeing, heard without truly listening, as Rose continued to pass her fingers across the keys of the piano. It was somehow discordant to my ears, the anger assuredly having leached from my own darkness into the girl, yet still the rage burned within me, civility all but gone. What madness overtook me then, I cannot say, but the veneer of my class was quite ripped away. Where decency and societal decorum should have checked my actions to this child, the responsibility of my position as one of benevolent gentry drummed into me from when I was but a child myself, etiquette, deportment and the unquestionable birthright that had placed me above other men, none of it – none of it could, none of it would hold me back in that moment. Rage burned, self-loathing, disgust at my infirmity and that cold nagging wish that I had not survived this bloody war all churned in my belly and blocked all sense, all light. Rage, pure and visceral.

Before I could stop myself, I had reached over

and slammed the lid of the piano down, missing the child's fingers by a hairsbreadth. I cannot recall the words that then passed between us, maid and master, but they must have been cruel, cold, an unacceptable breach and affront to how a man in my position should have spoken to a child in hers. But I could not call them back.

I stared down at my good hand and as I saw my fingers dig into her flesh, discolouring and bruising its pale perfection, an overwhelming sense of repugnance shook me back to sense. As if a viper had bitten me, I dropped her arm, I felt nauseous, unstable, and like a fool from the travelling circus I started to stumble and fall.

Blinking back tears the child inexplicably stood to aid me, ushered me to my chair and placed my cane in my hand only for it to fall again discarded at my feet. Dear God, what had I done? What kind of monster was I? This guiltless child had done nothing to injure me and I had behaved as a beast, abused my position and yet, and yet, she had shown me compassion, she had shown me charity. Gently, trying not to frighten her I reached for her hand. She locked her eyes to my gaze and what she saw reflected back must have calmed and reassured her that the madness had finally passed.

"I have no right to ask this of you. I cannot..." I stumbled and stuttered in my speech trying to force an understanding on her, asking for absolution though I knew I did not deserve it. "Forgive me, there are not words… I…"

She must have uttered a response, I know not what, but whatever it was encouraged me to proceed.

"Play for me? I do not command you do to it, but I would very much like to hear you play."

The music soothed and caressed in a way nothing else in my small world could. I bathed in it, feeling its balm touch my black and broken soul, giving solace, healing. And in my heart I made a promise, that never again would I let the beast rise within, never again would I let self-pity choke and unman me. I would somehow, some day, find a way to make it up to the girl, to win back her trust, to heal the wounds in her that I myself had made.

As she slipped out the verandah doors, I saw her brother race to join her, he must have been close by, he must have heard every word. Guilt washed over me anew as I comprehended how my actions had surely scarred them both, pitiful creature that I was.

CHAPTER 15

WHISPERS

William

Summer turned to Autumn, and we all trooped back to the school room for the start of the new school year. Rose at twelve was now one of the eldest children in the class, for my mother was firm that she should continue her education for as long as she was able to keep her there. By twelve, many of Rose's classmates had already been taken out of school, either to work in the fields with their mothers or to find employment in service.

To begin with I was eager to return to the little school in Long Wendon, but as the year drew to a close it became a torment to me and I would try every excuse to persuade my mother against sending me. I could not of course tell her the real reason, but she knew, of course she knew. My torment came in the person of Sean Martin, a boy of some twelve or thirteen years who was bluff and brave and big for his age, though quite slow at his letters for all his bravado and swagger. In short, he was a typical bully, who made up for his own shortcomings by picking on those who were younger and weaker, but were nonetheless intellectually abler than he.

'Cat got your tongue, Billy Baxter?' he would sneer as I ran past him to get into class – a reference to my growing reluctance to talk with any other save my immediate family. He would follow this up with a taunt to my sister; 'Simple is he Rose?'

'Not as simple as you Sean Martin,' she would quip back and set those who were nearby into fits of giggles. She was only trying to help, but it did more harm than good. Whenever he came across me unguarded, he would take great delight in a casual pinching, a wrist-burn or a dig in the ribs, daring me to stand up to him, which I never did. I just turned the other way, hoping he would tire of me, and start picking on someone else.

I started to hope that my tactics for dealing with Sean Martin were beginning to pay off, but then disaster – that's when the news about my father reached our little village. How it got out, I do not know, a casual whisper here, an unguarded remark there, but rumours have an insidious power to take hold and take hold they did, until every man, woman and child knew the sad and shameful truth.

It was one November morning and Rose and I had just entered the playground, all bundled up in our winter coats and caps for we had woken to a hard frost that morning, an icy, chilled wind and a shower of wintry rain. I felt the eyes turn on us directly as we entered the yard and there was plenty of whispering behind mittened hands. Sean Martin was standing with a group of older boys who were seemingly pushing him forward, egging him on.

"Hey Billy, come here!" he sneered. "I've got some news for you. See, I know all about your dad the war hero." Behind him the group of boys sniggered. "You'd best not tell your story anymore, you lying little runt, coz we know better, don't we? He turned his smiling eyes away from me and there was a murmured assent from the throng of children crowded behind him. "The truth is Billy your dad wasn't fit to tie my father's boots. War hero, is it? That's a funny one!" The crowd of circling children started laughing.

By this time Sean was towering over me, poking me in the ribcage with one of his stubby fingers. He was relishing every minute of the encounter, for he was sure that I was ignorant of the prized piece of information that was in his possession. And so I was, not knowing what to say, not daring to reply, just wanting it to end.

"He was a dirty, stinking coward Billy Baxter!" He jabbed the words as he jabbed his finger into my chest. "And you're just the same. You'll turn out a bad one just like him. And maybe they'll shoot you too!"

The words whirled about in my head as if searching for a meaning, but I could make no sense of any of it. Who? Why? Why would someone shoot my dad, shoot me? By contrast that secret knowledge, or the whisper of it at any rate had clearly reached the ears of my sister for all of a sudden, I felt her standing beside me, her face scarlet and her hands balled into two fists.

"Shut up, shut up Sean Martin! Or I'll shut your mouth for you," she said.

"Ho, ho, brave little girl aren't we? Braver than your daddy," he mocked in reply.

Rose took a step towards Sean, though he was a full head taller than her and screwing up her fist even tighter, she let it fly straight into his laughing face. He shouted out in pain and shock and when he pulled his hands away, we all saw blood spurting from his nose.

What happened next was a whirl of shouting and confusion. Miss Adam came flying out of the schoolroom, already hollering at Sean to go and wash his bloody face and hands. Next, she commanded the rest of the class to get indoors, take out their slates and set to work on the arithmetic problems that she had chalked on the board. The class trooped inside silently while Miss Adam turned her attention to Rose and I.

"Miss Baxter, what have you to say for

yourself? We do not fight in this school, no matter what the provocation."

"But he…"

Miss Adam cut her short. "No matter what the provocation. Is that clear?"

"Yes Miss."

Both Rose and Sean were punished and made to apologize for their behaviour in front of the whole class, and both felt greatly aggrieved at having done so.

When the school day was over, we did not go up to Grange Park as we would normally have done, but instead a quietly whispered instruction from Miss Adam sent us home to our cottage where my mother was waiting for us.

Rose rushed straight into our mother's arms. "Is it true Mum? Say it's not true?"

She stroked my sister's hair and shushed her soothingly. "Sit down Rose and you too Billy", she said taking my hand and pulling me to the stool beside her. With a heart laden with sadness, she told us of the visit she had received from the Reverend Hawkins, who in turn had shared with her the news that the Reverend C. White had imparted to him by way of a letter. There could be no sugaring of the pill. The news was the worst kind as she laid out before us every scrap of the story exactly as it had been told to her, of our father's desertion and still worse the manner of his death.

With the facts laid bare, my mother Lily struggled to make us understand the words she spoke, tried to make us see the wasteful cruelty of our father's death as her adult heart had seen it. My sister Rose caught her every breath, her every heart beat and with a lover's fervency she embraced my mother's steadfast belief in our father's innocence. I was left behind, drowning in a child's comprehension of the incomprehensible. With a blank face and a blank heart, I heard the words that my mother spoke, but I did not understand them. How could I? He had been a soldier I knew that was a fact. But how could it be that he was shot by someone other than the enemy? It made no sense to me. Rose, poor Rose, wept tears of pure rage, as determined in her belief in our father's innocence as our dear mother was. Should she be ashamed, should I? I could not fathom the whys and wherefores, no matter how hard I tried to turn it over in my mind. I kept silent; the words would not come.

"Always remember this, my dears, that despite what anyone says, your father was a good man. Now dry your tears Rose, for we must all be very brave. And if anyone should say a false word against him, you must turn away, knowing that they speak a lie." She held Rose's face in her hand.

"Do you hear me my girl? No more fighting. Do you understand?"

Rose involuntarily rubbed her knuckle, the one that had made such successful contact with Sean Martin's face. My mother took Rose's hand in hers, examining it. With a smile she mused, "You'll have a bruise there, Rose, just see if you don't."

I could not know it then, but am sure of it now, sure of the strength my mother showed us in her quiet words. How did she come in all the days that followed to greet each morning without the weight of sorrow and disgrace pressing down upon her and suffocating her breath? Every eye in the village must have been turned upon her, such was the stigma placed on those who had deserted, such was the condemnation meted out to all those who were associated with the deserter. Pity, revulsion, pride all played their parts in my mother's treatment and she bore it all without an outward sign of weakness. What was surely in her heart stayed locked away from the gossips and onlookers as she heeded her own advice to us children and simply looked away.

I did not have my mother's courage. That was the day my speech disappeared. As my understanding faltered and swelled, with it came the strange emotions of shame, sorrow, defiance and love. They followed me on my heel like shadows, and I chose to walk with them silently, not saying a word. I could not explain it to myself and so I would not explain it to anyone else. It was not a conscious decision, I know that now, merely something that happened and was curiously accepted by all those around me

CHAPTER 16

THE END OF THE WAR

William

1917 turned into 1918. Occasionally the daily routine would be punctuated by the return of a soldier from the front. But these men would not stay long, with only two weeks leave a year the largest part of that time was spent in journeying. There would be brief private celebrations and rejoicing before the war claimed them back. Many did not make the journey home, feeling easier in the company of their fellows, not yet ready to share all that they had known of soldiering in the Great War.

Summer melted into Autumn and life continued on its way. The days were not all gloomy, my mother's quiet steadfastness lifted our spirits and at times we reclaimed that sense of carefree joy that is the rightful inheritance of all children when the wind takes them. In September we filled our baskets with blackberries from the hedgerows, delighting in and coveting the foraged fruit that our mum would make pies and puddings with. In October we gathered the last of the fallen apples and placed them in wooden boxes and set them by for the turn of the season.

As November beckoned, the cold wet storms of winter brought with them a shift in the air. By the time the leaves had fallen to the ground around the lanes of Long Wendon we knew that the war was coming to an end.

Later, much later, we learned of the momentous events that had been acted out in the theatre of battle. We heard how the signing of the armistice had taken place with little celebration. Near the front lines, in a railway carriage parked in the forest of Compiègne, the terms of agreement were signed calling for the cessation of fighting along the entire Western Front to begin at precisely 11am on the 11th of November 1918. Many directly involved in the conflict, dug deep along the lines of trenches, had not believed that after four long and bloody years that everything could stop, that the armies could simply pack up their gear, disperse and the fighting men head home. Many had thought that this would prove to be a temporary halt, that it was not truly the finish.

Back home, by contrast, we heard sooner the stories of great rejoicing in the streets of London and up and down the length of the country, of flags being waved and glasses raised in thankfulness and relief. We did not know that it would take so long for the soldiers to come home.

Christmas came and went and there was still no word from my brother Tom. I had not seen him since the start of the war, and truth be told I barely could remember his face for he was one of the men who had not been home on leave, choosing rather to keep counsel with his army peers. Rose remembered more than I, and each morning she expected news that finally he was headed home. His anticipated return at any moment gave us all something to look forward to, it gave us too a counter weapon to the gossips' condemnation and whispered scorn. Tom in my eyes had grown into the status of a demi-god, so much had he been built up through my mother's and sister's reports of him that when he finally did come home, I was a little disappointed that he was not ten feet tall or more!

But his homecoming, when it came, was too late for our mother. Hers was a short and violent illness that took her off with almost casual cruelty. She died of the Spanish flu after displaying the symptoms for just a few weeks. The meagre diet of the war years had left her system weak to infection and she did not suffer for long.

My memory of the weeks that followed my mother's death were something of a blur. I suppose Rose and I must have been in a state of shock, not old enough to comprehend the scale of personal tragedy that had been indiscriminately heaped upon our family. A father and mother both gone and a brother God knew where and us children with no place to stay. Had it not been for the kindness of the Reverend's wife who urged and cajoled her husband to take us into their own home I feel sure we would have ended up in the workhouse. Our sister Susan would not have us, the excuses were thin as paper, she was with child, we might have the influenza ourselves, there was no room, the list went on. But the real reason was that her husband refused to take us on and we were to read into that what we would and he for one did not care. Poor Susan, her hands were tied.

Mrs Hawkins was very kind to us, she had not been blessed with children herself, but she was both diligent and thoughtful in her care of us and we were a pair of grateful grieving mice, subdued and thankful all at the same time.

I don't know how long we lodged at the vicarage, a few months, no more, but while we were there the wheels for our future security were set in motion. By the time our brother finally did come home Lady Mountfield had been persuaded to honour the pledge of employment for Tom that she had given to my mother shortly before her death. A small cottage on the estate was to be our new home. Lady

Mountfield had decided that her protégé should surely be rescued from her present straightened circumstances, and particularly as there was a brother old enough to care for us, once he finally returned from France, then everything would come out right in the end. Lady bountiful had fixed our futures without a word to us or our brother Tom – it was presented to him as a fait accompli upon his return.

CHAPTER 17

COMING HOME

Tom

It's April 1919. The colour's just starting to come back to the land after Winter and I'm finally headed home. I walk the last six miles back to Long Wendon. I didn't write ahead to say when I was coming, I'm not wanting any fuss. They'll know when I get there.

Things don't look so different here to what they did when I left. Over four years and I've not been back. I don't know what I'll find, Rose and Billy, Billy and Rose will they know me? Will I know them? Rose for sure, I guess, but Billy? I don't know.

I'm to go straight up to the Reverend's the letter says. And then I figure I'll see what's what. I'm in no rush, and I idle along the lane. It's nearly dusk and there's no-one about, and I'm grateful for it. I guess they're all at their suppers indoors. I shuffle along the lane a while further and turn the corner, past the church and into the church yard. I cast my eye quickly across the gravestones, but I can't make out the names so I go closer. In the corner by the north gate, I see a small head stone and I know it's hers. I go closer and kneel down. Lillian Baxter 1876-1919. There is no "in loving memory" carved, that would have cost extra and I reckon the parish paid for the stone. I lay a handful of wild daffodils in front of the grave. I picked them on the banks of the stream I passed an hour or so back – I forget the name of it. That done, I say a prayer under my breath. I'm not a churchgoer, but it seems right I should. I stand and turn towards the lights of the vicarage and walk on.

The Reverend himself opens the door to me, he shakes my hand and takes my pack, setting it down on the table in the hallway. From the open door behind there's a light shining from the parlour. The Reverend leads me through and there sit Mrs Hawkins and my brother and sister.

There's a clatter of chairs as everyone stands. Mrs Hawkins is fussing and coaxing the boy to step forward. But he's like a bloomin' statue stuck to the floor. "I'll not bite, Billy," I say. "Will you not give your brother a welcome?" Stiffly he shakes my hand and I ruffle his hair and he doesn't say anything. "Cat got your tongue?" I say trying to make him smile, anything. I catch a look that's thrown between the Mrs and the Reverend and I file that look away so's I'll remember to ask about it later. Then Rose is next to me. She hugs me awkward like, her thin arms don't go right round my back like they used to I've grown that much since I went away. She steps back. She smiles a shy smile and there're tears in her eyes that she wipes away quick.

"Welcome home Tom," she says, like she's all grown up all of a sudden, which she's not, but sure she's grown and is as pretty as ever she was, maybe more so. "How old are you now Rose?" I ask. "Don't you know Tom Baxter?!" she laughs "I'm twelve of course, nearly thirteen and Billy's eight, don't you remember how old we are!" She rattles on, she's that excited like.

"Hush Rose, where are your manners child? Your poor brother is likely tired from his journey. Now fetch him a chair and get an extra plate from the kitchen and mind you pile it high." She near hurls a chair at me in her hurry and laughing she's out the room in an instant to fetch me a plate. And I figure that Rose, my pretty sister Rose is like she's always been.

I sit down awkward like for the company's grander than I'm used to. The Reverend hands me a glass of ale. His wife doesn't like drink in the house I can see, but he makes a show of it, saying he had it by for when I'm home and he takes one himself to keep me company. The boy, my brother Billy I mean, keeps staring, it's like he can't take his eyes off me. "What's up with the boy?" It makes me uneasy.

"Nothing!" Rose is back and puts a plate before me.

"Eat up Tom, you must be famished," says the Reverend. "There will be plenty of time to talk later."

Rose chatters about this and that and nothing while I finish my plate and then Mrs Hawkins shoos her and Billy away. I can tell that Rose wants to stay, but the Mrs is stern and Rose does as she's told. As she takes my plate from me I give her a little squeeze on the cheek, and then I remember my dad used to do that. But Rose doesn't seem to mind and she smiles and goes out the door. Billy follows. I can't make him out. I guess he doesn't remember me. That must be it.

The Reverend's wife soon follows the children out and leaves me alone with Hawkins. I don't rightly know what to say now I'm here and so I sit and stare down at the fire in the grate. After a time, the Reverend coughs, polite like and I turn my head towards him. He is strangely ill at ease. He makes to apologize for his kindness, when it's me that should be thanking him for taking in my sister and brother when no-one else would, not even my own sister Susan. He tells me what's what and what I will do and where I will live and everything.

"Lady Mountfield has arranged it all Tom. For my part I cannot fathom the depth of that good woman's charitable and kindly acts, for she has surely made things right for Rose and Billy and your good self." The Reverend continues without drawing breath.

And so, my future is mapped out for me. The day after tomorrow I am to report to the house and start work. It's gardening work, and I guess it's as good as I'll get around here. I'm to work under Mr Frances, who I know is getting on in years and if I'm good at my job and hardworking and honest and the like the Reverend reckons, I'll get on right well. I can't rightly explain it, but as he says these words, I feel my world tightening fast around me.

We talk late into the night and I'm glad to sit at the Reverend's table and drink his ale. He is a good man I reckon, and I should be as grateful to him as I will need to be to Lady Mountfield when I come by her. And yet why do I feel that my life is somehow come to an end before it's rightly begun? My hope was to get away before the war came, before the army, and now my big grand childish plans are finished. I guess I should be thankful to God that I'm alive and out of the war, but the plain truth is, I don't know if I am.

I sit awhile longer, my gaze drawn back to the fire and my mind wanders back to Billy and how he just looked at me with his solemn eyes and wouldn't say a word. I'm a plain man and I see things plain and I want to know what's what, right now, right here with no fancy talking. I know something's up with the boy and I ask straight out.

"What's wrong with Billy? He don't seem right," I ask.

The Reverend takes a breath and it's like I see him thinking, the thoughts are clear on his forehead before his mouth says the words. "You think him changed?" He asks.

"He don't talk." That's me – blunt – I say it as it is.

The Reverend sighs. I've gone right to the point and he knows it of course, so he can't wrap it up in any fancy words. "It was when he found out about your father," he explains. "He just stopped talking. No-one really knows why."

The little fool's playing games is all, I think, but out loud I say sharp; "Can't anyone make him talk, damn it?"

"Force him to speak, shake it out of him you mean?" The Reverend sounds surprised.

"Yes, why not?"

"Your mother, Lily, wouldn't allow it. She said that he would talk when he was ready to talk."

"My mother said that. That's plain daft Reverend."

"No, no Tom I don't think so. Your mother was

nobody's fool. She knew what she was about, and I think she could see that Billy wasn't ready to talk about things."

"I don't follow you."

"Children can be very cruel when they want to be Tom, and of course none of them knew the exact circumstances."

"The other kids got at him on account of our dad? Why don't he stand up to them, fight back. I'll soon knock some sense into him, you see if I don't."

The Reverend looks startled. I feel anger, but I know I should keep it in, and I try to in front of him. The Reverend speaks more slowly, but earnest the way he thinks he should talk to me so that I understand his meaning.

"No Tom, no you must absolutely not do that. Just let him be. Besides, I don't think he's scared of them, though he is only young. No, I think rather that he doesn't have anything to say to them and so he won't waste his words. Your mother said that she thought he was working everything out in his own mind, and once he had, then he'd most likely talk again as if nothing had happened. And I think she was right."

"That's stupid, stubborn, stupid."

"No, no Tom. Not really. I urge you just to let him be for the moment and see what happens.

If you go about trying to frighten him into speaking, you'll only make things worse. Get to know him again. You're years apart in age and he probably doesn't remember you from before the war. Just get to know him again. What was he, three or four years old when you went away?"

I turn this over in my mind and then I say: "I'll let him be. For now, at least. But don't he even talk to Rose?"

"I don't know. They certainly communicate, but as to whether he speaks to her or not I really couldn't say."

"What if I was to pay some fancy doctor to look at him, would it do any good? I've got pay from the army, and if I have to spend that on him I will. I want him fixed."

"I don't think he needs fixing, Tom. Keep that money safe, you never know when you'll need it. Billy is all right. Just let him be. He'll talk when he's ready. Don't you worry. I'll bet my ministry on it!"

At that I laugh out loud. If it was a joke it was a poor one, but I laugh just the same. And then I think of Rose. She looked right enough, but I have to ask.

"And Rose?" I seem to startle him again, I think my manners are too rough for him, my voice all wrong, too loud. But it's the only one I've got.

"Bless you son, there's nothing too much wrong with Rose. She's a little headstrong and gets herself into scrapes at school sometimes and by all accounts she's got a good right hook for a girl, or so Miss Adam tells me."

"What?!" He says I'm not to worry and with the next breath he tells me my sister's good at fighting. I'll need to stop that quick.

"Nothing to be alarmed at, son. No, no, Rose is by and large a good girl, but she does have a temper on her, especially when she thinks she's in the right. But don't you worry about her, she's a resourceful child and I daresay a loving one too. She certainly looks out for Billy. And certainly, you know she's got herself quite a talent in her music..."

The Reverend talks some more, explains things like. I'm sure he's a bit worse for the ale, but he talks right on for another half hour more before we both turn in for the night. He tells me about Rose and her skill at playing the piano and the Mountfields and a good deal more besides. Playing the piano is it, I can't think what good that will do her, but I keep that thought private.

So much has happened in Long Wendon since I left. I find that strange somehow. When I was away at the war time marched on so slowly with the daily routine not changing much from one day to the next. But here, life has raced on at lightning speed and my brother and sister have changed so much from what they were. I don't know how I will fit back to this life?

CHAPTER 18

BROTHER AND SISTER

William

The cottage we moved to after Tom came home was on the estate. It was smaller than the one in the village, being no more than a room that was attached to an end row of cottages, with a small loft above. I think it must have been an addition because when you looked outside the stone was a different colour where ours joined to the next building. The row was filled with other workers on the estate, Mr Frances, the gardener was one and some of the farm hands shared quarters in two of the other buildings, but we were the only children.

Rose and I had a bed in the loft above the main room that you got to by way of a ladder and of course you couldn't stand up in it, not even me, but it was the warmest place, the heat from the fire would rise up to us on cold nights.

Tom had his bed made up in the corner of the main room, but there was plenty of space for the table, three chairs and the rickety old dresser that was filled with pots, pans, plates and such like. There were also a couple of thick wooden trunks with leather straps nailed round them. One was ours, mine and Rose's and the other was for Tom to keep his few possessions in. It suited us very well and Tom kept telling us we were lucky to have it and we should be grateful, though we both knew that without being told. But the best thing about our new home was that we were out of the village, away from the school and the village kids and were living on the estate. The walk to school was longer, but I didn't care and neither did Rose.

Tom was another matter. He was a poor substitute for the mother we'd lost. You knew where you were with Lily Baxter but since Tom had come back from the war, he was all brooding fists and dark brows. Rose did her best to play the little housekeeper to our brother, but she got scant thanks for her pains. For my part I tried to keep out of the way of this tall, broad man they claimed was my brother, for in this stranger I could trace no memory of the brother I once knew.

It fell to my sister to tend the house, to cook, to clean, to fetch the water and wash our clothes. But she did not complain, for there was no-one else to do it. Our brother kept a tight hand on the money he earned, and he insisted on paying in person for and collecting the food that Rose then cooked and put on the table in front of him.

Tom worked long days in the grounds, learning at the side of Mr Frances to tend and nurture the fruits in the orchard, to sow and crop in the vegetable patch, to cut the lawns and clip the hedges. He learned fast how to plan and manage the vast gardens around the big house and Mr Frances was well satisfied with his natural aptitude for the work and his readiness to learn. This was the one thing that I could not fathom about my brother, for when I looked on him, I saw a big burly man, broad of chest like my father had been with hands so large I thought they would surely crush the fragile plants that he was learning to tend. But they did not. Growing and tending seemed to suit his nature, dark as it was, it seemed to soothe him. It was if he knew where he was with the planting and sowing and nurturing of things that sprang from the soil, but with us I knew there was a gulf of circumstance and experience that kept my sister and I far apart from him.

I helped Rose with her tasks as much as she would let me, but we both still attended school and of course my sister still went up to Grange Park to practice the piano for the mistress of the house. I did not know at the time why this rankled so much with our brother Tom, but it surely did and woe-betide Rose if she was late with our brother's meals on account of her practising.

'Where have you been this time, Rose?' he would demand, knowing full well the answer. Most times Rose would say straight that she had been delayed through her practising, and that she was sorry, giving Tom the excuse merely to grunt and mutter about how he shouldn't have to wait after a long day's work for his supper. But on other days Rose would make the mistake of challenging him, saying that if he wanted his supper sooner, he should make it himself. On these occasions the anger and fire bubbled out of my sister in equal measure to the brooding anger of my brother and the stage would be set for a roaring row between them. If I saw the signs of an impending confrontation I would make my escape, scurrying up the ladder to the loft to be out of the line of fire.

The worst occasion I remember, happened two or three months after Tom had returned home and my sister had been kept longer than usual by Lady Mountfield at the big house. I could tell that my brother was in a black mood and so I made myself scarce in the loft, wishing my sister would come back soon for her delay only made things worse.

As Rose unlatched the door to our cottage, my brother was sat facing her at the table. He waited with his usual demand on the tip of his tongue, his brows knitted tightly together and a temper in his heart nurtured by a lack of food in his belly.

"Where have you been Rose?"

"You know right well where I've been, so why do you ask, now let me pass and get on with the supper," came her curt reply. She hung her coat on the hook by the door and snatched up the apron that was slung across the dresser. From where I sat crouched in the loft, I saw his back tense as the anger rose inside him.

"Don't speak to me that way child," my brother hissed, "I'll have none of your lip, do you hear?"

Rose roughly tied the apron strings behind her back and turned to stare at Tom. "What do you want me to say to Lady Mountfield? Well?" When she got no reply, she persisted. "That I can't come and play for her now that my big brother wants his food cooked and on-the-table as soon as he steps through the door? After all she's done for us, for you Tom? It's her that gave you your work. Her and no-one else. Certainly not you!" She looked him square in the eye, her face blazing with frustration and rage.

He rose from the chair and squared right back to her. He was a good deal taller than Rose and he towered over her when he stood, but she did not step back, not this time. "Listen to me girl and listen good, you were left to me to look after and you'll do as I say when I say, or you'll be sorry for it. I work long hours to keep you both and I didn't ask to do it. Mother and Father's gone and it's left to me and the least I deserve from you is to mind what I say."

"I keep the house for you as best I can, don't I? And all you ever do is snarl and spit at us, Billy and me both and tell us how grateful we should be to you and to the whole wide world, though it's as clear as day that you'd much rather not be here. That you'd sooner not have us to burden you." She'd hit the mark with that one, had my sister, for she had an uncanny knack of speaking in a way that showed her much older than her thirteen years. As I peered down on the scene unfolding before me, I saw her straighten her spine and lift her chin, and it was with a sinking feeling that I realised that she would not back down.

"I do mind you Tom, though I don't know as why I should sometimes you make it that hard for me and Billy. But I can't be in two places, there and here at the same time, and you're a fool if you think I can!"

"A fool is it, Rose, a fool?! You say you're sorry right this minute or I swear I'll teach you to mind me better, do you hear?"

My sister was right of course, she couldn't be here and there at the same time, but as soon as she'd called him a fool, she knew she couldn't take the word back. She stood there defiant, mute as he snatched her hand and squeezed her fingers so tight together that it made me catch my breath to see it. But Rose would not say a word.

"What's it to be Rose?" Tom's anger was equal to my sister's as he continued to squeeze 'til surely she had to cry out. "Say you are sorry, girl." As I watched from my spy-hole I saw clearly that he was the child, the bully in the playground as he pressed harder on her fingers, and she was the older and wiser sibling in this confrontation between brother and sister. And yet, stubbornly, stupidly, she would not yield.

She answered him in a voice as quiet as steel, "I'm not and I will not."

Tom let go her hands and she snatched them quickly away. He unloosened his belt and bent it double in his hand. "You will be Rose."

In that moment, all that I knew was that I could not let him touch her and finding a borrowed courage that was surely not mine to own, I flung myself down the ladder as fast as my legs would fly. Before he could lift the belt to her, before he could scarce know where I had come from, I hurled my body against him. I was like a feather hitting rock, but it took Tom by surprise. He blinked strangely and looked down at me and this gave Rose enough time to run. She pulled her coat from the hook, lifted the latch on the door and sprinted out into the night. My brother stared down at me, then stared at the door as it swung back on its hinge, bewildered. His rage vanished as swiftly as it had come. He dropped the belt and sat back down heavily in the chair. I did not know which way his mood would turn, and I surely did not expect him to do as he then did,to throw his head right back and howl with laughter. For a short while I thought that he had surely lost his wits, for I had never seen him laugh.

"A fool, is it?" he said to the room as the first tears of laughter began to roll down his face. "Maybe I am at that Rose Baxter, maybe I am at that." And then he stared at me again. "Mercy, our Rose's got a fine temper on her hasn't she Billy?" I studied his face, this stranger, my brother, who had so much violence and blackness inside him since he had come back from the war that it scared me to the core. My memory of him before was so dimmed by the passage of time that I wondered whether he had always been that way and I had just been too young to know it.

"Do you know where she's gone to?" He asked. I shook my head. "Will you not answer me, Billy? Will you not say a word to your own brother?" I knew my silence hurt him, and I was glad of it; I would not speak though he'd said the words kindly enough.

He picked up his belt from where it lay on the floor and buckled it round his waist. "Go and tell your sister she can come back, for I know you'll have a notion where she's gone." I eyed him cautiously. "Just fetch her home Billy, it's dark outside, just fetch her home." I hesitated as he sought for the words to convince me that he would not try to hurt her again. "I reckon she and I have said all we're going to say this night. Just run and fetch her. I'll be the one to make our supper this night." I nodded and went out through the unlatched door.

It took over an hour to find her and by the time we returned home, Tom had been as true as his word and the cottage was filled with the warming smell of stew. Cautiously he took Rose's coat from her as she stepped inside and hung it back on the hook. "Sit down and eat why don't you?" He ladled out the stew and put it before us on the table with a plate of bread and we supped in silence.

"What do you think?" he asked, his voice low and soft, quietened I knew for her.

"It's good," whispered Rose. We sat in awkward silence for a while and ate the meal my brother had prepared. When we were done Rose and I got to our feet and started to clear away the dishes.

"Leave it why don't you, I'll see to it. You'd best turn in, it's late." I was exhausted and needed no urging, but Rose was slower and as she passed our brother, he stopped her. He took her injured hand in his and turned it over to inspect the bruises that he had been author to. "I'm sorry for that. It'll not happen again." Just that, no more and my sister followed me to the loft.

Naively I expected this to be the end of Tom's dark moods. But of course, it was not, how could it be? For seldom does one single moment transform the nature of a human soul and certainly not one as wounded as my brother's. We had a temporary truce, nothing more.

CHAPTER 19

TOM AND ROSE

Tom

It's June, still light outside, though it's getting late by the clock and there's yet no sign of my sister. The boy I reckon is up in the loft or somewhere else fretting most like. I call up to see if he's there, knowing there'll be no reply. "Billy, where's our Rose got to?" He looks down from the edge of the loft and shakes his head. I want to shake him, but I won't. I remember the Reverend's words and my promise to that man to let the boy be. But his silence for sure puts a tightness on my chest and I can't shake that.

Though it's getting late, there's no fire in the grate and no supper cooking on the hearth and I'm weary and like a nag that cannot shoo the flies from off its face I have a temper inside me. I can feel the rage biting and I know my sister will see the worst of it. I know I won't be able to stop it neither and that's the truth. Damn it, why won't the girl come home? And I know the answer why, she's been up to the fine house to play her pretty tunes for the mistress. Why? God only knows. All

I know is there's a rumbling in my belly and Rose is not yet home.

To make the time run on I set to making a fire and put a pot of water on to boil. The time ticks by and I sit myself down at the table, facing the door waiting for the pot to boil and Rose to come home.

As she unlatches the door I am on my feet. "Where have you been Rose?" I want her to defy me and she does so in a heartbeat. She ties the apron round her waist, I can see she's weary and cross like me. "I'll have none of your lip, do you hear?" And the talk between us flies back and forth and I'm fuelling the fire and so's she, though she don't know that she does it, but she does. And the time races by so quickly, though the brooding took so long, and we get to the point so fast where neither of us will back down. She calls me a fool; she spits it at me.

"A fool is it, Rose, a fool! You say you're sorry right this minute or I swear I'll teach you to mind me better, do you hear?" But she won't take it back, she can't take it back and she's right, I am a fool, but I won't have it, not from her.

"What's it to be Rose?" I grab, then squeeze her small fingers between mine. She lifts her chin higher and I squeeze harder, hoping to squeeze a tear from her eye. But she won't give in to me. She's proud and stubborn like me. She won't give in. I beg, "Say you're sorry, girl". But she will not, and her next words bring me to the end point, the point that we've been heading for since she crossed the step this night.

"I'm not and I will not." She barely speaks the words; the sound of her voice is that soft. But there is no going back now and in my anger I will strike her over and over 'til she begs me to stop, and I may not stop then, for the rage inside me is grown too strong. And the thing of it is, I know in my mind that it's not about her, it's not about the want of a supper waiting, or her playing pretty tunes for the mistress or her pride. It's not that she defies me neither. I know it's not any of that. But she will pay for it, this anger inside me.

I've unhooked my belt and wound it round my hand and with the other I hold my sister by the collar of her dress and push her down against the table. I sense her fear, I see her pride disappearing, though she struggles to get free.

A moment later and she's gone, fled out the door into the night and in front of me is Billy who's just run at me with all the strength of a puff of breeze. But it's enough and my rage is gone. I stare at him in shock and then I laugh. I sit down in the chair and still I laugh. The tears roll down my face and I see my brother thinks he's staring at the face of a mad man.

When I find my voice again, I ask him; "D'you

know where she's gone?" It takes a long while for him to see I will not strike her now. I've gone past that passion. "I reckon she and I have said all we're going to say this night". And although it is not dark, I give the child the lie that it will be soon, and he follows on her heels to find her.

Later, much later, when my brother and sister have gone up the loft ladder to bed, after I have cleared the dishes and washed the pots and scrubbed every surface of our home clean, I sit in front of the fire. I rock back and forth and the tears begin to flow and will not stop.

CHAPTER 20

BROTHERS

William

Later, much later, I woke to the sounds of movement below. Rose was sound asleep so quietly, so as not to wake her, I eased myself over to the edge of the loft by the ladder and looked down. It must have been four or five in the morning, for though there was a gloominess to the light, there was nevertheless enough to see by. My brother sat at the table, a cup in his hand which he set down on the table in front of him and started to turn in slow circles by the handle. He stared at it intently as if his eye would trace every crack, every curve of its surface.

As my eyes adjusted to the low light, I could see that he had cleared away the plates and scrapings from last night and the crockery was now dried and stacked on the old dresser. The kettle was hanging over the embers of the fire, so clearly my brother had made himself a brew a little while before. I watched him cautiously, trying to determine his mood and it occurred to me then that perhaps he had not slept at all. I watched as he stood up and stretched, then moved over to the fire and started to prod and poke it back to life. He added a few sticks and two lumps of coal which was an extravagance at this time of the year and after a while the small, orange tongues of flame began to burn up from the embers and lick their way around the new fuel.

Content now that a small fire blazed in the grate, my brother sat back on his haunches and stared into the flames. By fire-light I saw his face and to my child's eye he looked curiously older than his years, a frightening face and one that I imagined to have seen terrible things. As I watched he suddenly hugged himself, as if a pain had at that moment gripped him in the chest, but it had not. He made no sound, no sob, but as I watched, silent tears traced the length of his face. I did not understand what I saw.

Slowly I crept to the edge of the ladder and as silently as I could I crept down into the room below. I walked into the light of the fire and stood before Tom, not quite sure how I had come to be there, my sense of purpose of a moment before now vanished. Tom looked up in surprise, hurriedly wiped the traces of tears with the back of his broad hand and instantly the emotion that I had just witnessed was banished. "Did I wake you, Billy?" he said as gently as he could. I shook my head. I wanted to say something to him. I wanted to say to him that everything was all right. That we were all right, but the words did not get past my lips, but remained in my throat unheard.

"Go back to bed Billy," he said. I turned and climbed the ladder again, all the while watching my brother. He smiled up at me and then lay down on his make-shift bed and closed his eyes. I watched him for some time silently still in the half light, but he kept the lids of his eyes tight shut.

After a while I turned my face away and instead stared at the spiders' webs above me as they glistened in the predawn light that now pushed through the cracks in the roof. What was I thinking? I couldn't explain it. I had acted on impulse. I had recognised something in my brother's demeanour that had made me look on him as I would have looked upon some wounded animal happened across in the forest and in that realisation, I felt in me a desire to aid that creature. It seems foolish now, as I look back on that moment through much older, much wiser eyes; a small boy wanting to comfort the grown man that my brother had become. And yet? I'm not certain. Would Rose have known what to do? I'm not sure. Perhaps she might, but right then she lay fast asleep locked in the world of her own dreams.

For a little while I watched a gold and black

spider industriously spin her web, taking care with every tiny thread, then before it was quite dawn, I must have drifted back to sleep.

CHAPTER 21

A BARGAIN

Edward

On my discharge from Kenny House, I busied my days with idleness and regret, and I dare say an unhealthy cupful of self-pity into the bargain. The unpleasant truth was that it was many months before I began to form any kind of interest to occupy my invalid days, for I had not the heart, stamina or purpose to push myself on. Curiously it was largely on account of my father's unexpected decline that I found myself drawn to finally take an interest in the world around me. Of all his sons, my brother Peter had carried the weight of my father's dreams on his back; of his three sons he'd most resembled him, he'd spoken like him, he'd acted like him and of us all, though he would never admit favourites, he was the son on whom my father had depended most. Peter was the son who would have carried the traditions of the Mountfield's into the next generation. He had been of the right stock, made of the right metal and his passing had left my father simply bewildered at his loss. He chose to absent himself more and more to his study like an uncomprehending child.

Thus, my own rehabilitation was brought about in part by the necessity for someone to take on the duties of running the house and the estate in his stead. Previously I had assumed that this would prove tedious work, but in reality it began to give me a direction to my days and moreover took me out of the house and away from the worst of my own dark thoughts.

Julia, of course, was a near constant presence at Grange Park these days and though I was resolved there could now never be anything between us, our friendship had strangely grown, not lessened as a result. I wished on occasions that she would find someone else who could give her what I could not, but her clipped responses to that sentiment whenever I expressed it, left me strangely comforted by the force of her continued denials. I think I truly wanted her to find another but was at the same time gratified that she had not. It was if another man would take both my lover and my friend. The lover I had long forsworn, she I had disavowed as I lay on my sickbed with the sound of falling shells still ringing in my ears, and the scent of earth and blood still in my nostrils, but the friend? Could I let her go? There was my reluctance. So, Julia had remained.

In the Spring of 1919, the Baxter children moved onto the estate lands with their brother

Tom who had recently returned from the war. This meant that we saw more of the girl up at the house as my mother now insisted that she came every day to practice. Her older brother Tom had been given the assistant gardener's job to Mr Frances and seemed, by all accounts, to be making a good job of the work and that left only the mute boy – Billy – who I would regularly see wandering about the estate. He was in nobody's way and indeed I felt sorry for the boy, for he seemed to be as lost in his world as I was now unfitted to useful purpose in mine. Tom Baxter, I could tell by his look, was a stern and straightforward man and I could guess that the life that the three of them now led was sober and austere and most likely without much joy and as result I was much softened in my disposition towards Rose, the child who had so enraptured my mother with her musical skill. But in my heart of hearts, I knew that it was not for that reason alone and I was but fooling myself to think otherwise. My guilt was often heavy when I thought of what had transpired between myself and Rose that long ago afternoon. My unjust treatment of her was no pardonable sin and I chastised myself often for having let my self-pity cast its ugly shadow so viciously upon an innocent.

Her talent, so out of place with her circumstance, was something to be admired and at the same time something to be pitied. For what possible use could there ever be in such skill and learning in one such as her?

It was on one Saturday afternoon in June when my shadow Julia, my mother and I were once again in the drawing room. Of late Rose had taken to approaching through the gardens and, on this occasion, she was accompanied by Billy to the delight of Julia who for some unfathomable reason was much taken with the boy.

"I shall take Billy for a long walk for it is such a pleasant afternoon and we shall learn the names of the early summer flowers that grow wild in the meadow." She announced this while snatching up a book as she moved towards the open verandah windows.

"You shall learn them, I'm sure my dear," I replied. "But are you not forgetting the boy is mute and will not be able to repeat one name back to you."

"Hush now Edward," she admonished. "He does not speak now, as you well know, but all that will change in time." Of course, the whole village had heard by now of the Reverend's theory concerning the boy's silence and there was even a rumour that a sweep stake had been started for those wishing to bet on the length of time it would take for the boy's speech to return.

"Edward, don't tease her." Lady Mountfield looked up from her reading. "She is generous to a fault with that poor lost boy, and why not I ask you? The child is motherless and perhaps the stimulation of her kindness will aid the recovery of his speech all the sooner. I must say that family have had their fair share of misfortunes, though," she continued.

"And between yourself and Julia you seem intent on compensating them to the full!" I replied irritably, instantly regretting my remark remembering that Rose was within earshot.

"It amuses me very well and even you must concede that Rose is a very fine music student."

"If you say so, Mother."

I watched Julia through the window as she walked away from the verandah in an animated, one-sided conversation with the boy. When she was with the child there returned in her some of the old carefree gaiety that had so enchanted me when first we met. It was a disagreeable thought and I brushed it firmly from my mind.

"You look tired Mother. Let me listen to Rose for you," I said. "It is a while since I've heard her play and perhaps you should rest?" I spoke a lie, for even when I was out on the estate, more often than not I returned to the house in the late afternoon only to hear the dulcet music rising up from underneath the child's assured fingers.

But today I was in a covetous mood and for some reason did not want to share the girl's skill with anyone else – not Julia and certainly not my mother.

"Yes indeed, Edward, if you wouldn't mind, for I have so many things to organise and I don't know where the time has gone today, really, I don't. That would be such a help."

I smiled in collusion at the thought of her so many and so unnecessary tasks as she left the drawing room, only the smallest part of me surprised by the speed with which she had taken up my offer. For she, like I, existed in a world of idleness, sheltered from all that was really urgent and necessary in life. I turned to the girl who looked at me with unreadable eyes. What was she thinking? That I would hurt her again? Once more shame washed over me from the memory. I needed to put her at her ease, dispel any lingering fear. I offered her a rictus smile.

"Please get out your music child. Why don't you pretend that I'm not here?" I said lightly, but the words were lame. Pretend I'm not here? No, the words were not lame, they were idiotic. Forcing my smile wider, I chided myself at my own foolishness.

Slowly she turned and seated herself at the piano stool quietly placing the book of music on the stand. She opened the page and creased back the book along its spine, selecting with care the piece that she would play. She began tentatively. I sank back into one of the armchairs and closed my eyes. I consciously made no sound, simply let the girl's extraordinary skill wash over me. The melody flowed faultlessly, rich and light and warm from her fingertips to the whispered end of the piece.

I opened my eyes and keeping my voice soft and encouraging said, "That was well done, Rose. Well done indeed." I walked across to her, noting the soft rise and fall in her chest as she sat on the stool alert with every breath. "Now is there another piece that you can play for me?"

She nodded and raised her hands to fumble with the music in front of her on the stand. It was then that I saw the yellow and purple marks on her right hand and I knew without asking that these had been inflicted by design. Without thinking I scooped up her injured fingers and turned her hand over in my own, ascertaining their extent. She flinched at the touch, but did not pull away; indeed, how could she, for was I not the master's son? "Do not be alarmed child," I reassured her. I awkwardly pulled up a hard backed chair and sat diagonally across from her. "Now, you will explain how you got these injuries," I said, once again taking her hand in mine.

"I don't know Sir." She bit her lip, defiant, still

sure of herself, still bolder than she should be.

"Who did this to you Rose?" I asked more forcefully, trying to look deeper into those black unfathomable eyes.

"It's nothing Sir. It was an accident," she lied, more cowed than I had ever seen her before.

"You will not tell me?" She shook her head. "Very well, then let me guess." She shook her head again more earnestly and this time I read the near panic in her eyes. I released her hand and she pulled it back into her own lap, unconsciously cradling it with her uninjured one.

"Then I will make a bargain with you child. I will keep silent, though I think you know that I can guess at the author of those bruises." Her eyes widened with a mixture of indignation and fear. "You know full well that if I were to say anything about this to my mother the person in question would surely lose their position." She knew I had possession of the truth and I dared her to gainsay me.

She lifted her chin towards me, her small body rigid with the effort. "What bargain Sir?"

"Are you afraid, Rose?" Her reaction amused me, but I was not yet finished with her.

"Should I be afraid Sir?" Her boldness had taken me by surprise once before and it did so again.

"Good heavens child, of course not! The bargain that I will make with you is this. I will keep your secret, though should it become a recurring incidence I will intervene..."

"Sir no! You mustn't. You can't. I know it won't happen again," she interrupted and as quickly fell silent, a realisation in that instant coming upon her as her eyes swiftly searched the floor, or her lap, anywhere so long as she did not gaze upon my visage.

Clever, clever girl I mused. Had she recognised in that moment what I had grasped? Did she equate my late offence to her with this new one from another? Assuredly she knew that both I and this new offender were equally guilty, equally culpable. Was this cunning or guile? Neither: I quickly dispelled the notion forcing my voice to gentle, for certain she was no such creature as I.

"Well then. Knowledge is the price of my silence child. That is the bargain I wish to make with you."

"I don't understand sir?" She had spoken to her hands but then lifted her eyes from under her lashes to look at me, for despite the inequality of our positions she was bold, inquisitive, intelligent and I had surely sparked her interest.

"Let me just say that you intrigue me, and I

want to understand you better, I want to know what lies behind that fierce stare of yours." I was toying with her now, and I wanted to provoke a response from her. "The whole parish knows that you and your brothers have had troubles heaped upon you this year past and yet..."

She cut through me, "Mum said to me when Dad died that I shouldn't cry, cos what's done can't be changed and she said there's always other people much worse off than us." It was a matter-of-fact explanation, almost cold. I did not, would not believe her.

"But don't you think that it is terribly brave to think like that?"

"It's not brave. It's hard sometimes, Sir, but that don't make it not true."

"But child your father? ...the circumstances in which he died...and then of course your mother dying so suddenly..."

Her eyes widened again as she understood my direction; for I was speaking of things that I'm sure everyone in the whole parish either took pains to skirt around or used against her family as a weapon of condemnation.

Without pause she came again with her reply, "Mrs Hawkins and the Reverend took us in and now we're here. Tom is back and we have a place and so we're not so badly off as we could be and..." She ran out of words.

"Well child, sometimes I think you are much stronger than I."

"How can I be? she blinked. "Sir, can I ask you a question?"

Oh Lord, what was coming? I looked back at the pretty child who was slowly turning into the prettiest young woman that I had ever laid eyes on. What was she now, thirteen, fourteen? I shook the thought away. "I would have a care what you ask me Rose, but yes you may ask me a question if you dare," I warned her.

By this time, she was standing up and had walked across to the open verandah doors. She turned to face me. "The Lady Julia is very beautiful."

"That is not a question."

"They say in the village that you are going to marry her." The words were out without a flinch.

"Be careful child."

But she had gone so far already and would go further. "Why won't you marry her, sir?"

"That is a bold question, Rose." I almost laughed. "But that is most definitely none of your business, nor the business of the village at large!"

"But, Sir, if she don't mind you the way you are, why..." she faltered realising her gross misstep.

The way I am? There was the rub of it –

even this motherless girl saw only the cripple. Is that what emboldened her? I looked hard at her but saw no sign of pity in her face. "I think that is enough Rose." Looking to put an end to the discussion lest I should say something I regretted I continued. "I think perhaps it is time you returned to your practice."

"I'm sorry Sir, I spoke out of place." She looked down at her hands and then stared wistfully out into the garden. "I just meant she's lovely Sir. That's all. I meant no harm, truly."

I snatched at a laugh and said more to myself than to the child. "Yes, perhaps she is." I steeled myself. "And no, you did not speak out of place."

"Sir?"

"I think that moment is passed." I pressed on quickly. "I regret…" I forced myself to continue, pushing through my discomfiture, my miserable chagrin at attempting to explain. A man full grown, explaining the unexplainable to this half child. "I regret most profoundly…"

She, of course, knew to what I referred and cast her eyes down. "There is no need to, Sir."

Crossing to stand beside her I continued. "Please look at me Rose." She complied. "There is every need and this most certainly needs to be said. I should have said it a long time ago. Your brother is under my father's employ and you yourself benefit from my mother's generosity, but your situation does not and should not mean that you are accepting of such treatment as your due."

She looked at me as if to determine the truth, then bobbed her head. "Thank you, I think."

"Will you play for me Rose?"

She returned to the piano stool and played a sweet country ditty that I had not heard before and I guessed that this was not on the approved list of pieces that my mother had supplied her with.

"What is that called?"

"I don't know sir. It's a tune they play in the village sometimes. When my sister was wed, I remember it being played by the fiddlers. I just like it, is all Sir."

"And you don't like the music my mother makes you play?"

"No! I like that too;" she considered the question, "I think I like that more."

"You practice every day and you are quick of study; I would have to be a fool not to see that. I do not flatter you when I say you have an unnatural talent and skill, but what I don't understand is why."

"Why Sir?"

"Damn it girl, I mean why everything?" At her

puzzled expression I continued in earnest, "Why do you practice so hard at something that surely can be of no use to you in your future life. Is it the attention you seek, praise from my mother?" I would treat her boldness with my own.

"No, Sir, I wouldn't do it for that. That would be stupid. But Sir," she continued hurriedly "I am right grateful to Lady Mountfield..."

"Ha!" I stopped her with a snort of laughter. "I don't give a damn whether you are grateful to my mother or not, but what I do want to know is why you apply yourself so diligently?"

I fully expected her to come out with some foolish girl's nonsense about the music being pretty and heavenly or some such foolish fancy. I certainly did not expect to hear the reply she actually gave, and it provided me with much to think on.

"I don't know if I can say exactly. It might sound silly to you. But when I play, I like to hear it most when I play it right. And when it is all right, every note I mean, it's like it's inside me that I hear it. And later when I'm somewhere else, doing something else I can close my eyes and it's still there." A pretty blush suffused her face, as if the words had spilled out before she could stop them, with a purity of passion that had surprised even herself. She stopped and shrugged her shoulders.

Though heartfelt, she clearly considered her own explanation lacking in some small part, unable to articulate in words with the same clarity as the act of her playing could, the skill of her musical accomplishment. And was it any wonder? How could she express the pleasure that her own playing awoke inside her, when she did not possess the language to explain that emotion? And yet in this roughness I could discern a raw sense and then I had it. Inwardly I chuckled, did my mother know that she had created and was nurturing a working-class aesthete? The notion amused me beyond measure.

"What are you laughing at Sir?"

"Never you mind child." I watched as she wrinkled her face with displeasure, assuming that I was laughing at her. Should I disabuse her? It seemed cruel not to. "Rose, I was not laughing at you. For what it's worth, I liked your explanation, it does you much credit child. Now, I can see your brother and Julia coming back. Please resume your study," I commanded. I sank back into the armchair and once again closed my eyes, the music uplifting and pure and healing; or was it the child? – I dared not venture too far along that course lest the closer examination of it should furnish me with feelings and truths that I should not own, still less act upon in my poor ravaged condition.

CHAPTER 22

MR SCRIVENS

William

The rumour in the village was that the schoolteacher's not-so-young young man would soon return to Long Wendon and once again take up his weekly position as piano master. And so it was that in the Autumn of 1919 when I was nine years old and my sister Rose was fourteen, having celebrated her birthday at the beginning of the Summer, Mr Scrivens came back to the village school.

I for one did not rejoice at the prospect of his return, for I remembered only too well his stern countenance and his strict teaching methods which he had applied so exactly to his students before he left for the army, and if truth be told even the bravest boys in the school were a little afraid of him. The very first Monday of the new term, punctual as ever, Mr Scrivens had arrived early and as we entered the school gate the dreaded piano master stood side by side Miss Adam with an alarmingly benevolent smile on his face.

Behind a cupped hand John Grant suggested that the music master's war experience must surely have 'scrambled his wits' for he had never looked to us so amiable before. This did not however take the edge off the trepidation I felt, for I feared what the intimidating Mr Scrivens would make of my progress. I was one of those who had not been taught by the piano master before his departure, but had begun to learn during his absence. I had received a rudimentary grounding from my sister Rose, along with three other children whom Miss Adam had selected for Rose to teach. She had also been set the task of continuing the tutelage of the older boys and girls who had started learning with Mr Scrivens, but they were all now long gone. Emmy White had gone into service for a landowner in the next county, Mathew Graham who had narrowly missed going into the army was now a grown lad of sixteen and could be seen about the village helping his father with his business, and Peter Wood and Bob Turner had recently found labouring work on a nearby farm. Arthur Wilkinson, the oldest of Mr Scrivens' pupils enlisted in April 1918 when he turned sixteen. He did not return.

Looking back, I now wonder how our schoolteacher made sense of it all. How she continued in her task to educate us through the years of war, as month by month the boys she had cajoled and teased and wrestled into the act of learning their sums and their letters, disappeared from her school room one by one. How did she not lose heart when the news filtered back to Long Wendon of her former pupils lost or wounded in the fight? How did she round the circle and face up to the randomness of those losses and how did she comfort their sisters and younger siblings left behind in her school room and not rage against the injustice of such and such a pupil lost? Why Arthur Wilkinson, who had been a sharp and articulate student, surely destined to rise above his farm labourer's roots and become a clerk? Why John Gordon, who played the fool and made everyone laugh, but could still barely write his name when he left the parish? There was surely not a one of us in that village, or anywhere else in the country that had not been touched. And as it was for us, so too was it for our school mistress Eliza Adam. Somewhere in the middle of the war the fight for her had become personal too, as she waited and watched and hoped that her unlikely suitor, the implacable piano master, would somehow be spared.

As afore mentioned, in the absence of Mr Scrivens, the task of tutoring the piano players had fallen to my sister. Lady Mountfield thought this an admirable solution, and to Miss Adam's mind this was a strangely comforting arrangement, for surely by keeping his position open, Mr Scrivens would... must return. The usually rational and sceptical young woman took this very fact as an omen and she held on tight to it with all her heart right up to the day that Mr Scrivens walked back into the school yard.

Miss Adam was however a realist and knew that Rose would not be able to teach the more gentrified and elaborate music that Lady Mountfield would have preferred. Happily, Lady Mountfield was astute enough to acknowledge this and instead ordered new music books for the school that contained largely simplified versions of well-known hymns. This choice of music suited us much better and after nearly two years of practice I for one was more than content to hammer out *All Things Bright and Beautiful* at full pelt on the keys, no matter that I could only play the right-hand notes.

It was a warm, clear September day when we all trooped in through the school gate past the piano master. Miss Adam accompanied him slowly to the school house and I noticed that he was walking rather stiffly on account of what I was later to discover was an injury that he had sustained in his right ankle soon after arriving at the front. It had been a minor wound delivered by a wayward fragment of shell, but it had laid him up for several months in a field hospital in France. They entered the school together and moments later Miss Adam reappeared promptly to ring the bell for the start of the school day.

We lined up in our queues, girls to the left and boys to the right, and then followed one after the other to stand behind our desks. The schoolroom was small and rather cramped, but the unusually large windows that ran the length of the building let the September light flood in and as the sun streaked down, without a cloud in the sky, it gave the shabby little room an air of warmth and comfort.

"Good morning children," Miss Adam intoned to us and we children in turn sang back in chorus the familiar reply; 'Good Morning, Miss Adam'.

"I am sure you are all as happy and thankful as I am that Mr Scrivens has returned to our little school safe and well..." Several of the older boys sniggered into their hands, but Miss Adam pointedly refused to acknowledge them, for nothing could diminish her feelings of joy and gladness on this day and so she continued without pause... "And will resume his instruction of the piano. I would personally like to thank Rose for all her help over these last two years in continuing as best she could Mr Scriven's work. Thank you Rose." There was a little pause and Miss Adam encouraged us all to recognise my sister's efforts with an impromptu round of applause. The class joined in with gusto, as my sister was universally liked, especially now that the likes of Sean Martin had left school, and Rose herself blushed with pride at this unexpected praise.

"Now Rose, Billy, Peter Barlow, Mary and Susan, you will remain indoors with Mr Scrivens and please be sure to show him your best efforts. The rest of the class will join me outside with your slates as it is such a fine morning, and Peter Smith don't forget your chalk." There was a shuffling of shoes, a scraping of chairs and a murmur of excited chatter as the majority of Miss Adam's charges left the room. I remained indoors with the rest of Rose's pupils and I remember only too well the dryness in my mouth, the sweat in my palms and the thumping in my chest as I prepared to do my very best for Mr Scrivens.

Despite my pessimistic expectations, we five spent an enjoyable morning with the piano master, who to my delight and relief was not a bit like the Mr Scrivens I remembered. He seemed most satisfied with our progress and was warm with his praise and encouragement, though our fingers slipped up a good many times. But to a one we played with heart and I think that Mr Scrivens was genuinely surprised at our progress over the last two years, for none but Rose, had set a finger to a key before that time. We were never going to be more than adequate players, but the church choir would never in the future be short of an accompanist.

When it came to my sister's turn, she chose to play a piece that Lady Mountfield had given her. I of course had heard her practice this melody up at Grange Park, but none of my peers had heard her play anything like it before. Her fingers raced up and down the keys with an expert lightness of touch as she followed the notes of a composition by Beethoven. It was an allegro from a piece entitled Piano Sonata No. 9 and there were a whole other series of numbers and words, which to my uneducated eyes meant nothing, and seemed far too long a title for a tune even as beautiful as this one was. But the music as Rose set about her task, was truly lovely and I watched with curiosity as Mr Scrivens sat back in his chair and closed his eyes as if he were breathing the music in, rather than listening to it. I could tell without him saying a word that he was impressed by her playing.

Finally, he opened his eyes. "Well done dear child." He smiled at her. "You have lifted my spirits beyond measure. Lady Mountfield has certainly been rewarded for her faith and generosity in bringing music into this schoolroom." Turning to the rest of us children, his mood undiminished, he instructed us to rejoin our classmates just as Miss Adam rang the bell for the morning break.

I raced out of the room as fast as I could and caught up with my friend John. We ran directly to the window underneath which was placed the one bench in the school yard and climbed atop it: on tiptoes we peered in through the window.

As Miss Adam walked back through the door, Mr Scrivens was already on his feet to greet her. "My dear Eliza I must confess that I am confounded by Rose's uncommon skill. She plays as one who has practised for far longer than I know the child has had instruction. She has accomplished far more than I could ever have dared hope for someone of her upbringing. I must confess that when first I learnt of the music that Lady Mountfield required these children to play, I thought it to be impossible. But to have found a one such as she, who possesses such a lightness of touch and most assuredly has such a rare talent, believe me, I do not know what to say."

"You really think that our little Rose is such a fine player?" pressed Miss Adam, caught up for a moment in the passion of Mr Scrivens' enthusiasm.

"It is the truth, for I declare that I have heard many accomplished musicians in my time, but not one to match her skill at her age. And yet I fear, dear Eliza, what will become of this talent? Her class, her social position, her gender, oh yes, perhaps her gender most of all, weigh heavily against her ever being able to employ this gift in any fruitful capacity. I do hope that Lady Mountfield has a plan for her future. I pray it is so." Mr Scrivens seemed deflated by this thought, the thought that my sister's extraordinary ability should come to nothing in the end.

"Well now, Mr Scrivens, do not be downhearted. I am sure as you say that Lady Mountfield has Rose's future mapped out. For as you know, she undertook the girl's instruction herself and she would not do so lightly I am convinced of that."

"Yes, yes, Eliza. I am in no doubt of it. That most definitely must be the case." The piano master rallied.

"And now tell me, Mr Scrivens, what do you think of little Rose's pupils? I do hope you are pleased with the children," continued Miss Adam.

"I am most impressed dear Eliza," replied Mr Scrivens, the weight from his shoulders now lifted. "But, my dear Miss Adam, you had promised to call me Albert, at least when we are away from the children. Don't you remember?"

"Albert, yes of course, but it has been such a long time..." she trailed off.

"Not too long, I hope, to forget the promise we made to each other," said Mr Scrivens, taking Miss Adam's hand tentatively in his own.

At the window John Grant and I continued to peer through the glass, on tiptoe, our eyes a pop with awe and glee. Overbalancing and falling backwards into a crowd of our fellow classmates John spilt the delicious news of our teacher's re-awakening romance. But of course, the two adults had heard the commotion and before John could finish the tale we were being hauled up by our collars.

"What are you doing rolling around in the dirt boys?" questioned Miss Adam.

"We fell over Miss," lied John.

Miss Adam gave him a knowing smile. "Fell over your feet did you, John? And you too Billy I assume?" Silently I nodded my reply. "Then might I suggest you play over on the grass and away from the windows before you do yourselves some serious injury," she continued.

"Yes Miss," replied John and I nodded my assent.

After the morning break, Mr Scrivens set about testing the aptitude for playing of the younger members of the class in order to increase the numbers of those receiving tuition now that he was to resume his Monday visits to the school. It was also made clear to Mr Scrivens that Rose would not only receive instruction from the piano master but she would, unprecedentedly continue to practice at Grange Park with the lady of the house. This was welcomed by Albert Scrivens as encouraging news, as he took it as a sign that Lady Mountfield had Rose's future well in hand.

As an afternoon treat for the class, Mr Scrivens consented to act as the school accompanist, and we all sang our hearts out while the piano master dusted off the cobwebs of his own talent and indulged his passion for playing. The war had given him little opportunity for practice, and he was glad simply to play, even though not everything we sang that afternoon was completely in tune.

CHAPTER 23

GOSSIP

William

In the gloomy post war months of austerity that seemed to accompany the returning soldiers to the shores of Britain, our small corner of this island had at least one joyous event to look forward to. The blossoming relationship between the schoolmistress and her piano master was played out in plain sight and their growing attachment scrutinized and gossiped about by the village community at large. When, in due course, Mr Scrivens finally proposed to Miss Adam, their prospective marriage was scrutinized and gossiped about all the more.

The cost of war in terms of human lives is by its very nature high, but the Great War ensured that a whole generation of young women left behind were destined to live out their lives as old maids. Nature would eventually correct the imbalance, but for the young women of the immediate post-war years this correction would not come soon enough for them. And so, the disparity of ages between Mr Scrivens and Miss

Adam of nearly twenty years was not even a consideration in their union. Universal opinion had elevated the lowly piano master, whose hair was thinning and greying round the sides, all previous faults and imperfections forgotten, into the most eligible of bachelors and Miss Adam was considered to be the most fortunate of young women to have snared such a catch.

To us children, we saw only the slightly awkward behaviour of the pair as they danced round each other so delicately in their gentle courtship. He was courteous to a fault, and she demure and independent to his advances by turns. Each jar of flowers that appeared on Miss Adam's desk was greeted with knowing smiles, each casual hand offered to her in assistance to pass through a gate or doorway, where none of course was needed, was duly noted and absorbed by us with a wink and a nod and each unguarded smile between them both was filed away by us with grins and sniggers into our hands. Prior to their inevitable engagement, the whole village talked and talked and kept on talking about nothing else as if they were the community's own property. Once a date for their union had been decided upon one might suppose that announcement would have stilled the gossips tongues, but no, the talking did not stop, it simply changed direction. For in the looming nuptials of Eliza Adam and Albert

Scrivens, the inhabitants of Long Wendon found a context to debate the wider issue of his majesty's soldiers who had returned to a country of high unemployment and of the pressing need to find them work. And who better to give up their jobs, jobs that they had so ably carried on throughout the war years, than the mothers and daughters left behind? Even the grand ladies and gentlemen who occupied the hallowed halls of Grange Park joined in that debate.

It was early October, a Saturday afternoon that is recalled to memory, as I was helping my brother and Mr Frances in the task of re-lining the pond before the onset of Winter. The fish were to be temporarily re-housed in a large tank brought in for the purpose, while the work took place. My brother and Mr Frances were in discussion as to how to proceed, looking again at the plans that Lady Mountfield had given them, as there was also to be a slight change to the layout of the pond that would be managed at the same time.

I drifted away to the edge of the pond and sat down by the box hedge, bored with the dull conversation and impatient for the process to begin, for I had been given the exciting task of helping to catch the fish and I was eager to begin. I watched my brother and Mr Frances for a short time as they walked up and down the length of the pond, getting it clear in their minds just exactly what was required. After a while, realising that more discussion was needed, my attention turned towards the house. At that moment Sir Peter, on a rare excursion for him outside the confines of his stately home, Lady Mountfield, Edward and Julia were returning from a walk around the grounds. Tea had been set out for them on the verandah, for it was a beautiful warm October day, and they walked over and took their places around the little table that was set out for the purpose. The sight of my brother and Mr Frances had immediately caught Sir Peter's eye and he stared at them for a few moments before addressing his wife.

"What the devil do they think they're doing? I thought you said that the pond was being started today," said Sir Peter.

"Yes, it is dear, I expect they are just going over the plans," replied his wife.

"Don't be ridiculous woman! They're just walking round the pond like a couple of fools. They don't seem to know what they're looking at. Look!" He gesticulated towards my brother and Mr Frances. "See, they don't know which way up to hold them! Damned incompetent that's what it is – are you sure they can even read?" Not waiting for a reply from his wife, Sir Peter barked at his son. "Edward, go and make sure they don't make a damned mess of it. Put them straight to it and make it clear that I'm not paying them good wages to stand about like a couple of village idiots scratching their heads!"

Edward got up slowly and walked across the lawn to the pond while my gaze returned to Julia and the master and mistress of the house. I watched as Lady Mountfield instructed one of the servants to pour the tea and there was a gentle clattering of china as the cups and saucers were passed around.

"It's your fault woman, I should never have let you meddle with this. You've confused the silly buggers!"

"Peter really, we have a guest." Lady Mountfield affected indignation at her husband's turn of phrase.

"Stuff and nonsense, the girl's practically one of the family and she doesn't care a stuff whether I say bugger or not, do you girl? Right, aren't I? Bugger, bugger, bugger. Silly buggers that's what they are!"

"I am not offended, I can assure you, Sir Peter," Julia replied, though she did not look entirely at her ease.

"There you see, she doesn't mind a jot," he continued triumphantly to his wife.

"Yes dear, I'm sure Julia is very forgiving, but all the same..." replied Lady Mountfield.

"But all the same, nothing! I should have got

Edward to deal with it. He's doing a fine job, by all accounts managing the place and I'll tell you that for nothing. But he's another damned fool of course... don't know why he won't set a date..."

I saw Julia blush, even at this distance from the verandah, and I despised Sir Peter Mountfield for causing her this discomfit. To my young eyes he was an educated man, he did not need to speak to her in the language of a farm hand. I was convinced he did it merely to provoke a reaction from his wife, rather than to embarrass Julia, but embarrass that gentle lady he most certainly had and I smarted for her sake as one who had been struck. I had, I think, a childish crush on the young lady, though not one of a romantic nature – no this was something much more precious and solemn for I had put her on a pedestal of my own devising as one of the gentlest and purest and kindest creatures on this earth. But then, I was a naïve and foolish boy who had lost both his parents in quick succession. Under such circumstances what child would not idolize such a one as she who had sought out this lonely, voiceless boy and given freely of her own love and care and heart in recompense for all his troubles?

I crouched closer to the hedge, feeling the leaves prick against my face, my knees pressing against the stones under foot as I knelt making myself invisible. I willed with all my might, eyes tight shut, for this coarse and arrogant man, who so offended me to retreat back into the house, back into the domain that he had sought solace in since the death of his son. My extraordinary desire to protect the lovely Julia from the vulgar excesses of the boorish Sir Peter Mountfield was of course irrational, idiotic, and yet there it was in all its childish, unfathomable passion, so deeply did I adore and venerate the girl sitting at that moment beside him.

"Billy?" Someone was calling my name. "Billy!" I heard again. "What are you playing at lad?" This time I heard the irritation in my brother's voice. "I thought you was going to help?" Reluctantly I left my hiding spot and went to aid my brother and Mr Frances.

CHAPTER 24

THE POND AND OTHER CONVERSATION

Edward

My father was in a belligerent frame of mind and would not be crossed on anything this day. Somehow, my mother, who had decided to try and rehabilitate my father as she would one of her projects, had persuaded him to come out into the garden. I believe he only acquiesced to my mother's badgering in order to be rid of her nagging and of course he was reasonably taken with my fiancée as a 'sensible girl'. Julia would act as a barrier from his wife's hectoring he must have supposed. But why she had bothered, was a mystery to me. For months after my brother's death, he had kept his own company and kept largely to his own rooms and it had, up until recently been an arrangement that had suited everyone. I had found the running of the estate to be a diverting one, and I did not want my father encouraged back to take this task away from me. Even my mother herself had professed to suffer from far fewer headaches since his self-imposed withdrawal from family life, so I could not rightly comprehend why she was so keen to draw him out again. But then that was the contradiction in my mother. She would not leave things well alone and I for one, wished sincerely that she had. It would, unquestionably, only be a passing dalliance to jolt my father from his grief and melancholy, but for the moment she would not be dissuaded from her grand plan. Indeed, we had seen more of my father over the last two weeks than over the last two years in their entirety.

After putting Mr Frances and Tom to rights on the orientation of the planned drawings I returned to join Julia and my parents. My father it seemed was determined to pursue the conversation in the same irritable vein in which he had started it.

"Who's that urchin walking towards Frances?" complained my father. "I do believe the damned boy's been spying on us. If I catch him again, I'll… I'll…"

Julia cut across him, "Oh no Sir Peter. Please that's just Billy. He means no harm. Look, he's going to help Mr Frances and the younger man there is his brother. I expect he was just waiting for them to get started."

I couldn't resist the opportunity to needle my mother. "Yes father, Billy is one of the Baxter orphans. We have the whole pack of them living on the estate these days."

"Eh, what?" exclaimed my father. "Pack of them you say. How many are there man? What have you gone and done now you infuriating woman?" He glared accusingly at his wife. "Damn it Lily, are we to be a refuge to all the poor of the parish? Woman explain yourself!"

"Tom Baxter is our assistant gardener, and the boy Billy is his brother and Rose..." she tried to explain

"Rose, damn it! Not that bloody girl again."

"Peter, darling – language."

My father rounded on her. "I'll damn well swear in my own house and I'll thank you not to correct me in public woman! I told you to keep your protégés away from me and if you don't, I'll give you fair warning I'll kick them right out of Long Wendon myself," he spat at her.

I looked across to Julia and realised that my interference had backfired. I had not really wanted her to see the rancour that had grown between my parents and was now on naked display on the verandah. I gave my fiancée, for that is what she had remained despite my desiring otherwise, a knowing look to hold her peace.

"Father, please, I merely tried to make a jest, but it was ill-advised, and I apologize for it. Mr Frances reports that Tom Baxter is a most able young man and a hard worker." My father, I felt sure would listen to my opinion, for his opinion of me of late had improved greatly by virtue of the fact that the estate had not yet been brought to its knees under my management.

"Ah very well – then I apologise too, to Julia," he added pointedly, "And the boy and girl, what of them?"

"Father, about the girl Rose, I was at first as sceptical as you. But you must concede that she has made fine progress under mother's tutelage and will if nothing else make a good organist for the church choir."

"Edward..." my mother began to splutter, but it did the trick for Father who threw back his head and roared with laughter.

"Church organist! Ha! Very good."

"My fiancée," I continued pointedly using the word, "is very fond of the lad Billy – a poor mute boy, but really no trouble and he has a quality about him, perhaps on account of his disability, that makes him unlike the common children."

"Julia, you are fond of him, are you young lady?" asked my father.

"Oh, yes. He is such a dear, gentle soul and I do believe I can in time help him to speak again, for the Reverend Hawkins has said that there is nothing physically the matter with him that time and patience will not heal."

"Well, my dear," replied my father "if you feel that way about the boy, then I'll not say another word. Good for you to have a project, eh my dear?" He smiled indulgently at her. It was curious to hear the warmth of his condescension to her, though it belittled her nonetheless. Perhaps, before their relationship had soured, this would have been the same voice he would have used to address my mother. Perhaps if she had understood this denigrating view of her actions all those years ago and not mistook it instead for a lover's affection and encouragement the two would not have become my parents. I was not an advocate of women's suffrage, I was born too late and too comfortably to entertain that notion, but I could see that he was patronising Julia in the same way that he must have patronised my mother for all her married life, and it was a strange realisation that left me peculiarly uneasy.

I was momentarily distracted and found that when I re-joined the conversation my father had moved the topic on.

"And what do you make of this school teacher business Julia? I've seen the man, and he is not much of a catch though in these times beggars can't be choosers?"

"I must respectfully disagree, Sir Peter, if the village gossips are right, they say that theirs is a genuine attachment, and the word is that the two were romantically linked before Mr Scrivens went away to the war," replied Julia.

"Is that so? And do you take much account of the village gossips my dear?" continued my father.

"No indeed Sir Peter, but I do feel that it is mean-spirited to assume the worst of a situation, when one does not know all the facts."

"Well said my dear. Then I shall hereafter consider the piano master the most eligible of men," he continued, if a trifle condescendingly.

I watched my fiancée closely, as with gentle forthrightness she met every attempt by my father to mock her arguments with irony and to praise her at the same time with what I considered to be false approval. I had realised long ago that my father was a man who believed implicitly in the superiority of his gender as well as his class and the idle tittle tattle of women was to his mind scarcely to be tolerated. And yet how should that be so? For his life upon reflection had been as unremarkable as the life of the woman who sat beside him and whom he now despised; my mother. And what of my life? Was this to be my fate too? Creature of self-importance I envied him his certainty.

At length the servants came to clear away the tea things and my mother and father retired inside, not unexpectedly to separate ends of the house. I was left with Julia who showed no inclination to follow either of my parents, but instead had become engrossed in watching the trio of Mr Frances, Tom Baxter and the boy Billy as they readied themselves about their afternoon task.

CHAPTER 25

CATCHING FISH

Edward

"I think I'm going to ask if I can do something to help," announced Julia.

This took me by surprise. "I beg your pardon!" I exclaimed. "Help how?" I persisted as I got up and followed her over to the pond.

"It looks such fun!" she said at length, her eyes smiling back at me.

"Do ask if we can join them, Edward," she urged.

"We? There's no 'we' in any of this Julia," I reminded her.

"Very well." And with that she went right up to Mr Frances and took the small net from his hand. "Edward and I are volunteering our services to catch the fish," she announced.

"Well Miss, it's mucky work and no mistake and if Master Edward should slip on the mud…"

His solicitude was like a touch paper to me.

"Nonsense Frances, I've a gammy leg, but I'm not in a damned chair yet! Now hand me that other net man and let us all make a start," I barked at the poor man.

"Yes Sir, of course Sir, I didn't mean to…" he replied in great consternation as he hurriedly searched around for another net.

"Yes, yes man," I dismissed his apology, a little chagrined at my harsh reaction to his thoughtfulness, "I know you didn't mean anything by it. Damn it man, don't look so damned embarrassed, let's just begin, shall we?" I ended decisively.

"Yes Master Edward, Sir. Here's a net for you Sir. I'm afraid there's not much to it Sir, but to wade through and scoop 'em up."

"Well, I must say Frances, that's not very scientific, you'll have them swimming in all directions." I sought to draw him in with the warm laughter of camaraderie.

Tom Baxter and Billy were already in the water, their trousers rolled up to their knees and the elder brother was now holding a hand out to Julia who had quickly sloughed off her shoes and pinned her skirts up above her shins by tying the length of fabric into a knot at one side.

"Master Edward's right Mr Frances," Tom called out. "What if we all stand in a line and walk up together?" he said as he helped my fiancée into the water.

"Now that's a sensible plan, Tom!"

"Oh Edward, the water's surprisingly warm," remarked my fiancée.

"I'll be in directly," I replied. Mr Frances assisted me with the removal of my shoes and socks and the rolling up of my trousers, for in truth these things could not be quickly accomplished with a stick in my hand. He then set about removing his own shoes without a comment and as I stepped uncertainly into the green pond water I wondered for a moment if I would later regret this enterprise as folly.

"Quiet and steady as you can," said Tom and with those words we set out across the little pond in formation, sweeping our nets with one hand and I steadying myself on my cane with the other. We would surely have made a comical sight to any stranger coming on us unawares.

After the first turn, Tom sprang forward to take our nets and empty them of their catches into the waiting tank. I was grateful for this for it meant that I did not have to shift in and out of the pond for after only a few turns of the water my leg began to ache from the exertion. But it was no matter, I felt useful and in good company and that was more than compensation for the discomfort.

It took over an hour to scoop up all the fish

from the pond, for the task was far trickier than one might have thought. Billy out of us all, slipped the most and on several occasions his brother had to set him upright on his feet from having nose-dived headfirst into the green algae. Julia delighted in the boy's wild childish enthusiasm, and we all laughed heartily at the sight of the lad emerging from yet another slip wearing a green lily leaf just like a bonnet atop his dripping hair. Even Tom, who by reputation was said to be a sober young man, found much to laugh at in the child's antics.

By the end of the hour when all the fish were finally caught, Tom helped first my fiancée and then myself from the pond. And then Julia and I, walked back to the house. Billy insisted on carrying our shoes for us, before running back at full speed to help out with the rest of the work.

CHAPTER 26

FISHING WITH JULIA

William

There was no sweet music coming from the house that day for Rose had begged leave from the mistress to visit our sister Susan who lived in the next parish. It was three years past since Michael Crawley had moved his young wife away from Long Wendon, accepting a position just outside Broomfield on Lord Forrester's estate and I could not remember the last time that we had seen our sister. But this had been a special occasion, there was a new arrival in the family on account of Susan's second child having entered the world and Rose had been invited to see her new niece. She had offered to take me with her, but I barely remembered my older sister, having been only three when she was married and we had had precious little to do with her since she had become Mrs Crawley, and besides I had considered that splashing around in the Mountfield's pond would be a much better use of my afternoon.

Rose, however, had set out early that morning on Mr Brewster's cart to the next village and had intended to then walk the rest of the way to Susan's place, about three miles further along the road. She was to stay overnight and the plan was for her to get a ride for at least part of the way back with one of my sister's neighbours after Sunday Service at Broomfield. Susan had called her daughter Tilly, which sounded a funny kind of a name to me not having known anyone called after that name here in Long Wendon. Her son, who was five when his sister was born, was named Michael after his father.

"Billy?" I heard someone calling me. "Billy!" I heard the voice again and this time knew from the impatience in it that it was my brother's. "What are you playing at lad? I thought you was going to help?"

I took one last look at the party on the verandah and concentrated my attention on the task in hand. I rolled my trousers up as I hopped and raced back to the pond and then I eased my toes into the water, quietly, stealthily so that I did not disturb the fish. You can imagine my delight when the lady Julia decided to join us in our task accompanied by the stiff creature who was her fiancé. Edward Mountfield was as unsteady on his feet as a new born lamb and he moved awkwardly in the water which did nothing to smooth his progress, his face was set as a grim mask. I wondered whether he wished to please Julia by his actions for he did not complain in spite of the pain that at times I saw writ on his face. Sometimes I looked sideways at him and I thought I saw a shoot of pain take him – the sign of it only a slight grimace followed by a weary smile behind the eyes that he thought no-one took note on. But I saw it and maybe I thought better of him for it.

For my part I set about my task on that day with selfish joy. My brother too, was not so severe as he was accustomed to be, as if the water had softened his hard edges and all about us as we worked in unison laughter threatened to break out, though we tried to keep as quiet as we could.

Finally, all the prized fish were caught and temporarily re-homed and I clambered out of the pond and sank down onto the warm paving stones and wiped my muddy face with my wet and muddy sleeve. My heart raced with the exertion and although the sun had dropped lower in the sky to let in the chill of a late October afternoon, surprisingly I did not feel the cold.

Before Master Edward and the lady Julia could stop me, I had scooped up their shoes and carried them back to the house. As I waited by the verandah doors for them to approach, I watched my brother walking closely by the side of Edward Mountfield, the master all the while asking conciliatory questions on how Tom had settled in. I observed how he allowed my brother to take some of his burden. No words had been spoken, no aid offered and none solicited, and yet this sight was a strangely comforting, companionable one to my young eyes. In later years I was to see a painting such as this sight inspired, one not of servant and master, but of two brothers, the one leaning on his compatriot – two soldiers retreating through the muddy troughs of Passchendaele.

My recollection of that day as I look back through the lens of time is one of absence – of chords un-chimed and notes un-played. For as we splashed and squelched our way about the Mountfield's pond, my sister's music did not rise and fall on the breeze to accompany us as it was used to do most days now. Instead, we were left with only our own sounds as harmony: dull, rhythmic sounds; of slopping and slapping and warning shouts from Tom to have a care.

CHAPTER 27

PREPARATIONS

William

Rose returned from her to trip to Broomfield brim-full with the joy of renewing her relationship with our sister Susan and delighted at having seen the new arrival. According to Rose, Tilly was as sweet and placid a child as you could ever imagine. She recounted importantly how the infant at just a few weeks was sleeping through the night, which her older brother Michael had certainly never done, and that was indeed truly remarkable according to Rose. My sister had been deeply impressed by Susan's new life and had described in great detail the comfortable home in which Susan and her growing family were happily installed. Like us she lived in a tithe cottage on the estate of her husband's employer, but there the comparisons ended. Susan's home was like a palace to Rose's eyes in contrast to our most humble of dwellings. There were two separate bedrooms and two further rooms at the front of the house. "Imagine, I slept in a room all by myself, I felt like a queen!" she recounted, "And when the candle was blown out and I was snuggled up tight in my blanket all I could hear was my own breathing. I tell you it felt right strange to be on my own without another soul in the world."

Rose had found Susan's husband much older and stricter than she had remembered him being at our sister's wedding. Indeed, it had been several years since Michael Crawley and his young bride had left to live on Lord Forrester's estate and although the distance in miles between Broomfield and Long Wendon was small, our straightened circumstances and the rumours of stigma and disgrace had been enough in Michael Crawley's eyes to keep Susan apart from us. Rose was under no illusion that this separation was in large part Michael's doing, but at the same time she suspected that if our sister had really pressed the point with her husband he would have agreed to her meeting if only irregularly with her younger brother and sister.

The invitation to go to Long Wendon had come not long after Tom had returned to the parish, and Tom, angry and resentful at his sister for neglecting Rose and I in the intervening years and moreover when we most needed Susan's support, had at first been opposed to a reunion. 'You was not good enough for them before I came back Rose, so how can you be good enough for them now? Are you all of a sudden respectable like, now I'm home and working and you're no longer taken in for charity's sake?' Tom had argued on many an occasion. Finally, however, Rose's persistence had caused Tom to have a change of heart, and although he would have nothing to do with Michael or our sister, he would not prevent Rose from making the trip herself.

We spent several long hours that night listening to our sister chattering on merrily about all she had seen and done, and all that Susan had become and how our little nephew was faring and the like, until Tom and I were quite exhausted with the listening. But I do remember that night as being an unusually happy one in our home, when there were no cross words between my brother and sister and the mood was, if not exactly warm, somewhat lighter than it had been of late. As we sat round the table finishing our suppers, Rose's chatter inevitably returned to the topic that had engaged our neighbours and betters alike since the piano master had returned to Long Wendon. She had news and she was burning to share it.

"What do you say Tom? Mr Scrivens has finally asked Miss Adam to wed him. And it must be true, for I hitched a ride for the last mile back home with Mr Graham and he says it's the truth and no mistaking."

"What do I say Rose?" he answered with a nod to me, "Well I say he's no picture to look at, that's what I say."

"Oh Tom, why do you have to be so sour all the time?" she replied.

With a smile on his lips my brother answered, "I'm just saying she could have done better that's all. The man's too old for her by twenty years."

"Don't say that, Tom. It's lovely really and Miss Adam, she does so like him."

"Well sister, you're a fool of a girl with foolish ideas of love, and know no better, is what I say," retorted my brother as he wiped his plate with a piece of bread and popped it into his mouth satisfied.

At school the next morning the talk was all of Miss Adam and Mr Scrivens, and on account of it being a Monday and the usual day for the piano master's visit to school, we children were some of the very first to be told officially of their engagement.

Before lessons began, we all filed into class and were treated to a most solemn announcement by Mr Scrivens himself. Not accustomed to addressing the whole school at once, and perhaps being a little embarrassed on account of the news being of a personal and intimate kind, Mr Scrivens visibly reddened as he spoke to us.

"Children, as you all know, Miss Adam and I have for some time now, as two grown adults may be accustomed to do... What I mean to say is that Miss Adam and I have an understanding... an understanding of a most private nature. I mean I have made a proposal... a proposal to which Miss Adam has favourably indicated her acceptance..."

By this juncture, Mr Scrivens was positively scarlet in the face, and he took a pocket handkerchief out and began to pat his forehead down. Fortunately realising that her betrothed was floundering before her charges, Miss Adam, stepped forward, and quietly looped her slender arm through that of Mr Scrivens.

"Mr Scrivens and I are to marry my dears, and we thought it only best to tell you our happy news as soon as we had agreed matters between ourselves. In doing so we hope to put pay to all the whisperings that have been occurring in the school yard for many a long month. Yes, Jessica and Mary," she admonished, looking directly at the two girls sitting in the front row, "you two are some of the worst culprits for spreading your gossip." The two girls looked down red-faced into their hands. "So now of course there is no need for talk. In short, we plan to marry at the end of term. This little school and the pupils in it have been so much a part of my life, and latterly too of Mr Scrivens' that we hope that you and your families will all celebrate with us."

There was for certain no need for any kind

of formal invitation, this was to be a village wedding and as such it was assumed that all would attend, and all would pitch in to make it a happy occasion.

As you might imagine, it took a long while for the usual business of the school day to happen after this announcement, and needless to say the talk and gossip and whispering most definitely did not stop.

CHAPTER 28

WINTER 1919

William

As October turned into November the leaves, that had clung so resolutely to the trees during that long Autumn of uncharacteristic warmth and sunshine, finally began to change their colour and fall. Rain and wind had swept them down as if overnight so that by the first Sunday Service in November we filed into church over a carpet of frosted leaves.

On the 7th of November the King had issued a proclamation which called for two minutes silence to fall on the second anniversary of the cessation of hostilities on the Western Front:

All locomotion should cease, so that, in perfect stillness, the thoughts of everyone may be concentrated on reverent remembrance of the glorious dead. 1

So it was, in accordance with the King's decree and alike with settlements the length and breadth of the country, that we held our peace on that crisp Thursday morning of the eleventh of November 1919. Miss Adam had read out the Kings' words to us with a solemn heart and at the stroke of the clock the school room had fallen eerily silent. With that proclamation the adult world had entered at the door as even the youngest of us thought of the faces now absent from that place. All had been touched, none spared.

The following Sunday brought more returning soldiers to our parish as had been the case over the last few months and in particular I noted the presence of my brother's former friend, Daniel Martin. I confess that on sight of him I had anxiously scanned the pews in the nave to see if my tormentor was also in attendance. But he was not, reason dictated that it was folly for me to consider this a possibility, for Sean Martin had moved over a year ago to another parish where he had found employment as a labourer.

Daniel Martin was a tall man of near six feet. His hair was dark, neither mouse nor brown, and was cut short to his head in the army style. Some would say that he was a fine-looking man, for his jaw was square and his looks fresh with a clear complexion and there was not the smallest trace of the privations that he must have endured as a four-years-long served armourer of the kind that so haunted my brothers' features but for all that I did not like his face. There was a coldness in his eye that I could not quite discern, a confidence in his swagger that felt too fluent and a ring in his broad laugh that made me uneasy. He was deep in conversation with my brother as we left the church that morning, Rose and I, following at a pace behind. "Let's cut across the field," whispered Rose, slipping her arm through mine and with a quick nod to our brother we took a right turn down the lane to the stile gate.

When we had passed into the field Rose asked me what the matter was. I shrugged of course. "You don't like him for his brother's sake?" she asked. She read my assertion with a sigh. "You can speak to me Billy," she continued, as much to herself as to me, and I felt my stomach tie itself into a small knot. I regretted that I was not able to talk to my sister and I regretted it the more today having seen the look that Daniel Martin had cast in my sister's direction as we sat listening to the sermon. The thin smile with which he had appraised her from head to toe had had a meanness to it, if emotion in a person's intent can be so discerned. Rose had not noted his appraisal, for she would surely have blushed to the roots of her hair, for though I make no boast in saying that my sister was blossoming into the prettiest of young women, she certainly did not think of herself so and was not one prone to vanity. For, had she not been well schooled by our mother in years past, to know that a fair face could cause a poor girl more than a rich one a whole wealth of unlooked for troubles?

As we crossed the lower field out of the corner of my eye, I caught sight of a giant puffball mushroom and straightway raced toward it, Rose following with wild excitement on my heels. I pulled up short as I reached the spot where the mushroom was growing, disappointment clearly evident on my face as I noted the colour was no longer pure white but turning already to yellow. Rose stopped beside me. "Never mind Billy," she soothed. "Maybe we'll find others nearby." Then there was a flash in her eye as her face lit up with the idea. "Might as well kick it why don't you?" she encouraged. "It's no good to anyone now. It's turning rotten, see." She pointed to the yellow that was turning underneath to brown.

With one almighty boot I took a kick at it and watched with silent laughter as the spores exploded from its' heart. I crushed the fine powder-like middle and dull sponge-like flesh into the ground with the weight of satisfaction.

"Come on," said Rose at length. "Let's see if we can find others." I met her smiling eyes with a grin, grabbed my sister's hand tightly in mine and together we rushed across the crystal glazed, frosty field, over the next style, past the brook and emerged at last panting and out of breath in the lower meadow that bordered the Mountfield estate. My palm, where I held my sister's hand fast was clammy with sweat, but my breath still froze as I exhaled, mingling with the cold bitter air.

We pulled up all at once, Rose pointing to a faint patch of whiteness more prominent than the frost that dressed the rest of the meadow all over. "Look," she whispered, "it's a fairy ring." An unbroken ring of white field mushrooms completely encircled a corner patch of the ground. "Go quietly and you might see fairies Billy."

I shook my hand free, for I was not a child to believe in magic anymore, but it was certainly a sight to marvel at, for although not rare, fairy rings appeared seldom, and there was certainly a natural magic to their formation.

Rose ran a careless hand through my hair. "I wonder how it grows like that?" she whispered as she began to walk round the rim of the circle. "I guess they're all linked up somehow underground," she continued.

I shrugged.

"It seems a shame to pick them and spoil the ring," she said as she started to gather them into a fold she had made in her skirts. "Still, they'll most likely be gone by tomorrow, so we might as well take what Nature has given."

I smiled in agreement and started to help with

the gathering.

When we got back home it was nearly noon. Rose unlatched the door and we found Tom already seated by the fire which was ablaze in the grate.

"You took your time in coming," he admonished, but it was no more than an observation.

"We found a fairy ring in the lower meadow," Rose replied as she emptied the contents of her skirts onto the table.

Tom got up and went to check our haul. "They're good to eat, are they?" he questioned.

"Course they are. We checked." She held up a mushroom for our brother to inspect. "See! They've not even started to turn. What, d'you think we're daft Tom?"

"No Rose, never that," he laughed. "Too clever by half sometimes," he continued as he turned to wink at the man who occupied the other chair by the fire. In our rush to show Tom the mushrooms, neither Rose nor I had noticed the man seated in the other fire-side chair when we entered the cottage. It was Daniel Martin of course, Tom's former friend before he went to the war. "I've put the soup on to reheat, why don't you two set the table and put out the bread, and I think there's a bit of cheese left, isn't there Rose?" Tom asked. "Why don't you add a few of those mushrooms to the pot, that way it'll go a bit further as we've a visitor."

I set the table while Rose saw to the stretching out of our mid-day meal with the addition of the mushrooms. My brother sat back down and resumed his conversation with his friend. It was filled with enquiries about former acquaintances of the two, of whom I had little knowledge, but the talk all the same was suffused with the warmth of reminiscence and I seemed to discern a lightening in my brother's usually stern countenance, as the pair spoke nostalgically of times that went before.

"…I remember you got into a deal of trouble yourself with Mr Horner, Dan, never mind Ben Cranshaw. You weren't as blameless as you make yourself out to be now."

Daniel smiled. "D'you not wish sometimes you could go back to them days, Tom?"

"That's fools talk, Daniel. We can't none of us go back and I daresay we shouldn't want to knowing what'd be to follow if we did."

"Hark at you, a philosopher now is you, Tom? I just meant we had some larks back then, is all."

"Reckon you're right at that," replied my brother as he cast his eyes towards the fire. "So, what's for you now? Will you stay?"

"Nothing's fixed yet, but I hear there's the

chance of work out at Broomfield. I stopped in to see Sean on the way through to see if there's anything to be had that way." He turned with a smile to my sister." I heard how you bested my brother Rose, though not from his own lips I'll vouch you."

My sister was fixing the height of the pot hook as Daniel addressed her, and I could see even in the reflected light of the fire, how she flushed at his words, her cheeks twice red from the heat of the fire and the heat of Daniel Martin's remarks. The man drew pleasure from her blushes, I could see that.

"Now don't you fret, pretty Rose, for I heard as much as he deserved it, even from some of his own friends. You were sticking up for you and yours and the lad o' course," he continued with a nod in my direction. "So, no harm done, eh Rose?"

As she passed between the two of them, he half stood and reached for her two hands. "Now let me look at you, for you were just a little girl when I left and now, you're near full grown." This drew more blushes from my sister as she stood as mute as I before him, not knowing how to react.

"Nay, I'll not tease you no more girl, but you'll not mind my lack of graces, seeing as I'm Tom's own friend."

"O' course she won't, will you Rose?"

"No, I'll not, but I'll thank you to let go my hands now so as I can get food to the table."

Daniel did not release her hands at once but looked at her in mock solemnity. "Tell me what you will do with these hands and I'll let them go."

My brother laughed loudly at this, which brought on more blushes from my sister, but she lifted her chin just a little higher and looked Daniel Martin straight in the eye. "I want to use my mind, Mr Martin, not my hands. Miss Adam says I've the nature for it. I want to teach."

"And where do you think I'll get the money for that," exclaimed my brother flatly. "You'll go into service next year, or don't you remember we're poor?"

Daniel had let my sister go by this time and she turned to face Tom in earnest. "There's a training school over in Bedford and when I'm older that's where I want to go and…"

"That's enough Rose, it will still cost good money we don't have," he cut her off sharply.

"But Miss Adam says that…"

"That teacher shouldn't be filling your head with dreams and such that can't happen. Now hold your tongue girl and set the food on the table."

Rose turned away, smarting as if she had been struck, but I knew that look. I could see it in her eye as sure as if she had spoken the words, if there was a way, then Rose would seek it out.

I watched Daniel Martin closely in the lull that followed this exchange. He looked with curiosity at my sister as she fetched the heavy pot off the hook, clasping the hot handle with a rag with her too delicate hands. The steam rose and coloured her forearms where she had rolled back the sleeves, fine slender arms that should not be put to work in the service of others at washing and polishing from daybreak 'til night fall. I looked at the long straight fingers of her hands, hands that could play such sweet music, hands that should not be used in the mean or rude service of others. I felt angry at my brother and angry at Daniel Martin for having provoked this sudden outburst of enmity between my brother and sister.

CHAPTER 29

RETURNING FRIENDS

Tom

I nearly don't catch Rose's nod as she looks to pull Billy away, over the stile and across the field.

"Where they off to?" asks Dan. Daniel Martin, it's good to see him, though it's been nearly five years since I've set eyes on my friend. Like me, he's no longer the boy he was before the war came. He was always tall for his age but looking at him it seems like he's outgrown us all.

I scarcely believed it when I saw him sat there in church this morning, and now he's standing next to me as large as life. I'd heard he'd bought it two years past. Just goes to show you shouldn't pay much mind to other folk's talk. Often times when there's no news folk get to spinning half-truths – as likely to make up their own than say nothing at all if it makes 'em stand tall for a moment in the sight of others. I heard it all through the war, men who'd lived, men who'd died and those who'd come back like they was bleedin' ghosts, not dead at all, just lost in the mess of it all. And all on account of what some folks say 'bout others that's no kin to 'em, but feel a burning on their lips to spin a tale like it's the truth of the pulpit.

"Tom, what you staring at? I said where they off to?" he says again.

"Sorry Dan," I smile.

"Here, pinch me, I'm real," he jokes.

"Come back and eat with us, we'll make it stretch," I say.

"Thought you'd never ask. So, where's your sister gone?"

"Across the meadow. I reckon they'll not want to hang around while you and I chew over the past. We're old to them now," I add.

"Old, is it? – you're nought but twenty-two, you're one of the lucky buggers and so am I. Right thankful I am, I'm not one of the King's glorious dead! You should be too," he laughs and gives me a mock punch to the side of my head.

"Hey?" I shrug his hand off, but gently.

"Come on," he laughs. "I'll race you," he shouts and starts off at a run.

"Wait up you idiot, you don't know where." You can't fault the joy in him. I can feel it rubbing off on me, though I know my own heart's heavier most days now than it was used to be.

"Then catch me up," he yells behind him.

I break into a run, catch him and keep pace, my lungs filling up with the cold air snatched in. It's a mile or two to where we stay, but the distance falls away under my feet. He's at my shoulder, blowing hard. We're like the boys we once were each trying to get the upper hand on the other.

We slow our pace and step into a walk at last as we round the top of the hill and move along the track to where the houses stand in an uneven row.

"So, this is home?" he asks, stopping in front of the door.

"For now," I answer, though it don't feel like home, though I can't fathom full why.

We stoop under the lintel and Dan takes up a seat next to the hearth as I try and rekindle some life back into the fire. We don't talk. The cooking pot's waiting to be hung on the hook and when there's flames flicking up again, I set it on to heat.

"You look tired," Dan offers.

This gets a snort in reply and some of what's in me spills out before I can stop it. "You reckon, do you? I guess it's this place, that and the fact that I have my brother and sister to look out for now. There's no-one else, so the weight's on me. Damn it, Daniel. Of course I'm tired. I work and I sleep and I see my own dreams running away."

"Whoa, steady, Tom." He doesn't expect that. "Dreams?" he asks.

"Boy's dreams, that are no more, no less than that now." I ease down into the chair opposite my friend. "It's good you're back." And I'm glad of it.

"Seems a long time ago, don't it Tom? I remember now, you was all set to pack your bags and set sail to America or maybe Australia. The war's over, so what changed Tom?" he asks.

I stare at him as if he's simple. "It can't happen now," is all I say.

"Why not? On account of your brother and sister, is that it?"

"I reckon so. They're mine to look out for now."

"But not for always, Tom." I hear his irritation with me. "I can see now why Rose and Billy would think you're old. It's because you're talking like you are," he laughs. "A few years and they'll both be gone. Rose is of an age near enough now. And if she weds in a year or two, she can take the boy, take her turn at looking out for him."

"I'll not burden her with that, Dan," I say flatly, and I mean it. "Do you know, no-one 'cept the church man and his wife would look out for them when our mum died. Not even Susan; I've not spoken to my sister, nor had sight of her since I went away."

"You know that'll be her man's doing. You should make peace with your sister."

"I reckon." I look down at my hands, it's hard to say. "They were taken in for charity's sake Daniel. I feel like I'm beholden to the Reverend for that, and it's like everyone here is watching for me to fail – fail like my dad." I stop and punch my fist at the air, it's not coming out right any of it.

"Listen to yourself, Tom! Most everyone's in the same way as you. Some worse. Don't think on it so much. You'll do what you'll do and as for your dad? Don't think on that neither. The war's turned everything upside down and who knows what the right of it is. Listen to me Tom Baxter. Your Rose is nearly grown. It'll only be a few years and you can go to bleedin' Australia, to the moon if you like."

"There's a good many won't look at my sister for our dad's sake, Dan and you know it!"

"That's fool's talk, there's plenty men round these parts who would take a pretty girl like Rose in a minute no matter if her kin's related to the devil himself. Listen, I for one would take your sister and wed her tomorrow. And I'll take the boy as part of the bargain. What do you say to that?"

"She's nought but fourteen Dan – she's too

young yet. And anyways, why would you want her? You've not set eyes on the girl for five years."

"Maybe I've just taken a shine to the look of her. And why not Tom? She's spirit I can tell and why wouldn't I want to wed my friend's sister? I said I'll take her and I will, just see if I don't."

I let this pass, for he means well I reckon, but I know that his are only words. I know there's a deal of trouble set by for my sister on account of all that's gone before, on account of what men say, but I let that pass too. We fall into silence until Rose and Billy are back at last and we can get on with the business of making our meal.

CHAPTER 30

NOVEMBER ON THE ESTATE

Tom

It's been a week since Dan Martin returned to Long Wendon and it looks like he's set for staying, at least for a while. He's biding with us until he finds somewhere else to stay and I can't say I mind the company. It makes a change to Billy's silence and Rose's notions. She's taken to badgering me about the schooling so much that I've a mind to go up to the house and ask the mistress if there's the chance of work for her. That would soon put a stop to her grand ideas. The only thing that's stopping me is my own pride, I guess. I don't want it to seem like I'm taking advantage of her good nature, for hasn't she already set us up right well. It was because of my putting a word in that Dan's now working here on the estate. It's not for good like, but it's work nonetheless, helping me and Mr Frances with lifting and laying the slabs outside the back of the house where the family spend most of their days. It's heavy work and I can see that Mr Frances finds it hard graft so he's glad of an extra pair of hands, him being near sixty years in age.

The whole back area is to be dug up and put back down, though I don't fathom the why of it, for I'm sure it's not needing doing, excepting that it's Lady Mountfield's order that it be done. So, we set our backs to the task. Mr Frances don't say much, which suits me fine, but when he does talk his is a soft, gentle voice and Lord does the man have patience. He knows his place, never questions, just sets to, for he knows that what the Lady says is like the Bible truth. His hair has turned white over the years he's worked on the estate, pouring his heart into the tending of the gardens, like he loves them as his own. It seems strange to me to fix your life's work on gardens that have no use but to look pretty for them that owns the house and are free to cast their eyes on them, but he seems content, you'd not know to look on him that he's had his fair share of troubles. His wife and son both went to their graves nearly twenty years past, and his only daughter left the parish a while before that and he's lucky if he sees her but once a year.

All his thoughts are now for this rich lady's gardens. I swear he loves every inch of the place and every damn plant in it, he minds them with that much care. His hands, though a little crooked with age and most likely with arthritis, are small for a man's, though locked in those hands is all his skill. At times I'm sure that as he teaches me how to tend the plants, he's trying to teach me how to love them too. It's not boasting to say that I'm getting on right well, but I can't seem to learn the loving of them plants the way he would have me do. I can see the value of the onion sets, and the cabbages and the like that we plant in the vegetable garden. There's satisfaction there all right, put his blessed camelias and campanulas and such, I says you can't eat 'em so what's their worth?

We've been at this work all day, with Dan and I lifting and toting the slabs and there's still a deal more of them to go. Mr Frances has been barrowing sand back and forth; you can see the sweat on his brow as he works though the cold is starting to bite. It's getting dark now, though it's not late, it's just that the light fades quickly at this time of year. As we all stop to take a breath, Rose and Billy come round the corner of the house. They're back from school and I reckon Rose is heading to see her ladyship. She smiles as she sees us sat down taking our rest, Billy just stares cautiously.

"Hello Mr Frances," she calls, but casts a look in mine and Dan's direction as she comes by. Billy sets down on the step beside the old man.

"Hello Rose, my girl, and how was school my pretty miss?"

"Nay, Mr Frances, don't ask her that. She'll have

your ears pinned back for more than a half hour with her talk of schools and schooling."

Rose glares at me but holds her tongue.

"Well, I can't say it's done her any harm, she's certainly able to please the mistress with all her playing of them fancy tunes. That's where you'll be bound right now, I reckon, Rose?"

"Yes, I've to practice 'til six she told me."

"Well, well, you'll make a fine piano teacher yourself one of these days, and t'would be better wages than you'll make from being a lady's maid or seamstress, dear me yes."

"She'll not if I have anything to do with it."

"Why Tom, are you against it?" asks Mr Frances. I have surprised him.

"She'll stay here where I can keep an eye on her. I'm not wanting her gallivanting off to some man's fancy house to teach his young 'uns the piano."

"Why not Tom?" Rose asks then quickly returns to Mr Frances. "I don't think I want to teach piano Mr Frances, but I do want to teach and Miss Adam, who's soon to be Mrs Scrivens as you know, said I should if I went to Bedford and...."

Before she can run on any more, I cut her short. "That's enough Rose, Mr Frances doesn't want to be worried with all your talk."

"But…"

"I said that's enough. Can't you see that we've a deal of work cut out before we're finished tonight and it looks like Billy here will have to set to with the cooking if you've to go and please the mistress. Go on now. Billy you can stop a while with us. Mind you don't dawdle on the way back home Rose."

She turns on her heel and marches right through the open patio doors and into the house as bold as brass.

Dan Martin claps me on the shoulder. "Lord, is she head strong. Did you see the way she whipped her pleats round and planted her nose in the air."

"I saw." I reply sourly.

Dan laughs. "So, what have you got against her being a school mistress?"

"We're labourers Dan, and all the women in our family have been maids and seamstresses like Mr Frances says. It's what we know. The sooner I get her sorted out with a position the better."

"She'll not like it." Dan replies.

"She doesn't have to like it; she just has to do it."

Dan snorts back a laugh.

"You'd best finish lifting that last row, and then we'll call it a day," says Mr Frances as he rises and stretches out his back.

We fall back into the rhythm of the work and after a short while we hear Rose playing the piano, the music travelling through the open patio doors she has just walked through. I see a smile spread across Dan's face, for he has not heard my sister play before and he nods in my direction. "She's a fine player, and no mistaking."

"She is that Dan," Mr Frances agrees. I close my eyes. They have the right of it o' course. The music flows, too sweet for my taste. Grand folks' music, not of my knowing, not of hers neither, but the playing of it is still sweet for all that, but I fear what this skill will bring her, where it will take her.

We lift the last slab and stack it neatly against the wall with the rest. "I'll finish up here Mr Frances," I say.

"Right you are Tom. I'll see you tomorrow then." He smiles at Billy and, slowly laying the barrow on its end, he begins to walk off in the direction of the village.

"Dan why don't you and Billy go on back and make a start on the supper. See what you can find that Rose has laid by."

I watch them make their way across the field, in silence, damned if I know if that boy will ever talk.

I collect the tools that lay scattered round and about and all the while Rose's music hangs in the air like, it sounds that sweet that it near makes my eyes water to know it's my sister that's playing it. I put the tools in the bucket and pick up the spades and walk away from the house to the store. Returning with the broom I begin to sweep the loose soil and sand off the patio flags. My sister's music still steals out of the house and it's like it's an angel that's playing it and not my sister at all, though I know all the while that it is. I can see through the open doors that it is the young master that sits listening. As I finish the sweeping and stop to listen myself, he comes and closes the doors, shutting me out I know. I nod my head to him as I must and he turns away.

CHAPTER 31

PIANO PRACTICE

Edward

"Come in Rose," I said raising my eyebrows. The girl was already standing in the middle of the room, having come straight through the open verandah doors. Her face was flushed, and I saw that there was still a certain degree of pique in the girl's demeanour.

"Have you had cross words with your brother?" I had witnessed their little exchange through the window and it amused me in no small measure to see the girl holding back her sense of self-righteousness in front of her betters.

"No Sir," she replied.

"No?" I feigned surprise. "Both you and I know that that is an untruth." I waited a moment before continuing and was rewarded by a second blush colouring her cheek.

"Come, Rose and play. For you know I am teasing you. I'm sure you will say that this quarrel with your brother is none of my affair."

"I would say no such thing, Sir," she replied. "But since you know already, I shan't need to say, do I?"

"You are in danger of forgetting your place again, Rose" I observed wryly, "And the correct grammar is 'I do not need to say', not 'shan't need to say'. You can't use 'shan't' and 'do I' in the same sentence and for what it is worth 'Do I', is barely English at all. Are you learning nothing at school?"

Her eyelashes fluttered down to her feet at my rebuke. "Enough of this girl, I am not angry with you, but as is often the case only intrigued. Now, as you can see my mother is not here, so you will have to suffer me as your tutor, though I have no great aptitude and certainly own neither yours nor even my mother's proficiency at the instrument. However, we will talk later of your quarrel with your brother, but perhaps not now while he is stomping around the verandah."

At this she lifted her eyes away from their view of my mother's fine Chinese rug, and with almost a smile asked, "Shall I get my music out now, Sir?"

"Of course, child, and for heaven's sake play well, for I am in no mood to correct you." With this I eased myself down into one of the comfortable arm chairs and placed my cane lengthways across the small mahogany side table that stood at a right angle to the easy chair.

It was not long before I closed my eyes and let the music as balm soothe away my insignificant cares. There was no denying that the child had made excellent progress under my mother's tutelage and with the additional input from the recently returned piano master it was clear that my mother's recently expressed wish for the child to perform some kind of recital for her society friends was perhaps not as ridiculous an idea as my father had naturally, given his disposition to be opposed on principle to all my mother's projects, declared it to be.

My attention was distracted momentarily by the girl's brother who was now sweeping the verandah. I rose stiffly and with the aid of my cane I walked across to the doors. He noticed my approach and tipped his head in deferment as I knew he would. I closed the doors silently and returned to my seat and all the while the exquisite music swelled clear and pure from under the girl's finger tips, like the finest chilled wine suffuses not just the palate but every sense. I closed my eyes once more.

Rose played on for half an hour more: different pieces, some rousing, others melancholy but all approached with the same lightness of touch that was now instantly recognisable as the child's developing style.

The momentary silence that followed the girl's playing was my cue to reopen my eyes. From the angle that I was sitting, I could clearly discern the glow that now flushed her skin. I supposed this rosy blush was due to her gentle exertions as had she not put her whole body into the task of playing? Or perhaps I was mistaken in this, and it was not the effort at all but simply the music itself that had caused the reddening of her cheek, the tincture in her lip and the brightness in her eye. Surely the music had worked its magic on the player no less than on the listener. Her fingers had come to rest lightly on the keys, indicating a halt, but I was reluctant to break the spell they had woven.

Sensing that she was observed she turned her head.

"You played very well, Rose." My words in no measure did justice to her skill.

She turned her body on the piano stool to face me. "Thank you, Sir," she replied.

"Now, Rose, you will tell me what you and your brother were quarrelling about and we will see if there is anything that I can do to remedy it."

"You, Sir?" she queried cautiously.

"I am your brother's employer after all, child." I paused. "I am waiting."

I sensed her confusion, almost as if she were

trying to weigh the seriousness of my offer.

"We were speaking of when I'm to leave school, I mean what I am to do when I leave school, Sir," she said, rising from the stool and coming to stand directly in front of me. She barely paused in her answer, before blurting out. "My brother wants me to be a house maid, Sir," she said wrinkling her nose.

"I would say that was reasonable employment for a girl such as yourself, but I judge from your expression that you do not."

"Oh no, Sir, not at all. I would hate it, Sir."

"Ah, then we have a problem," I smiled.

"You're laughing at me, Sir." Her chin jutted out just a little in front of her now.

"By no means, Rose. Tell me, child, what is so wrong with you becoming a maid?"

"Nothing, Sir. 'cept I don't want to be one."

"And what do you want to be?"

"A teacher, Sir, like Miss Adam," she said simply.

"Your brother does not approve of your ambition?"

"No, he won't even listen to me. He says we've not the money, but Miss Adam says that there's a secondary school in Bedford and it's not so very far. If I got some work and saved real hard before

I go, for I know I can't go before I'm eighteen so I guess there'll be time... but he won't listen," she added, deflated.

"I see." I paused again. "Why do you wish to be a teacher, Rose?"

"Miss Adam says I can. She say's I've got the learning for it. And, oh, I don't know how to explain it Sir, but I want more than to clean up and make beds after rich folk all my life." She stopped abruptly, her cheek colouring afresh as she realised what she had said.

"Go on, child," I quickly encouraged. "I know you did not mean to be impertinent. Tell me, for I truly want to know."

"I don't mean that there's anything wrong with being a maid Sir, but I know, I just know I can be more."

"You sound like an ideal recruit for the Suffrage movement Rose," I teased.

At that moment my mother and Julia entered the drawing room and were clearly party to the end of our conversation.

"Eh what?" exclaimed my mother. "Our little Rose join the Suffrage movement? I think not, that would be appalling!" she continued.

"As usual Mother, you have interpreted wrongly. I was only teasing the poor girl. I doubt she's even heard of Mrs Pankhurst and her set."

"I have Sir," Rose interjected and then bit her lip.

I raised an eyebrow at this, clearly there was more to this rural mouse than met the eye. I chose to ignore her remark and persist with my explanation to my mother, for here, perhaps, was an ally for the girl.

"Rose wishes to become a teacher, but I do wonder," I said returning my attention directly to the girl, "Whether you have thought this through. When you marry child, which surely you will, you will have to give it all up. So, my question is this; why strive for that accomplishment in the first instance, when all is to be wasted in the end?"

Rose measured her words before she spoke, "I may marry, Sir, but also, I may not. I think it would be a fool who would wait around for something to happen that might not happen; and a fool who would not even try to better themselves when they could do it."

"Well said, Rose," interjected Julia. "Women have already proved themselves well able to do men's work whilst their husbands and fathers have been fighting the war, as you well know Edward. Perhaps in the future it will be perfectly acceptable for a woman to work after she is married."

I laughed heartily at this. "My dear Julia,

you are a positive delight sometimes. Perhaps I should be signing you up to the Suffragettes."

"The world is changing Edward, dear, all you have to do is open your eyes and look around you," replied my fiancée.

"Well, well, we will see about that in the long term, but in the short term I think you will find that, in Long Wendon at least, things are not changing as fast as you suppose, my dear. The rumour in the village is that once they are wed, Mr Scrivens will become the new school master."

"Miss Adam will not be our teacher?" Rose appeared a little taken aback. "But why?"

"Because as I have already taken pains to point out. Women do not work once they are married," I replied.

My fiancée put her arm around Rose's shoulder. "That is the case now, Rose, but when you are a teacher, perhaps the situation will have changed," she said gently.

"Do not go filling her head with fanciful ideas, Julia," tutted my mother. "There is plenty of time for Rose to be worrying her head about such things when she is grown."

Not exactly an ally yet then.

"I'm sorry Julia, but I for one think that it is only right that the women in our society make way for our returning heroes. You are seeing it all over. The women are returning to the hearth and the men are taking back the jobs that they vacated on account of the war. As I said, it is only right." I turned my attention back to the girl. "Do not look so down-hearted Rose. If it is a teacher you want to be and it is within our gift, then a teacher I am sure you shall be, if only for a little while before some young man turns your head and makes you his wife."

Ignoring my assumption that she would one day marry, she asked solemnly. "You really think I can?"

"The question is, do you?" I replied.

CHAPTER 32

NEWS OF A RECITAL

Edward

After the girl had gone, we settled down to our own private pursuits. I poured myself a drink and stood for a while at the verandah doors, nursing both a single shot of whisky and the ache in my leg that had been exacerbated from sitting too long in one position. The drink took the edge off the pain, but did not have the power to dull the sensation entirely and so I was never tempted to drink to excess. Indeed, after three years I had learned to live with my injuries, they were ever present, but I had discovered in myself the resolve to avoid wallowing in any kind of indulgent self-pity. What was done was done and I was well able to accept the inconvenience for what it was.

Julia had seated herself on one of the large wing-backed chairs and had her nose in the latest Wodehouse tome. "What keeps you so engrossed my dear?" I enquired knowing full well she hated to be disturbed whilst reading but was in the frame of mind to irritate.

She did not rise to the bait however, but instead set aside her book and came to join me at the window. "My Man Jeeves," she volunteered as she hooked her arm through mine, "as you are undoubtedly well aware."

"And do you find Mr Wodehouse amusing?" I asked condescendingly.

"Evidently, and so do you," she remarked pointedly, "for I have often seen you take a peek at my reading material when you think no one is looking."

This response elicited a smile from me, as she had most certainly intended.

My mother by this time had seated herself at the piano, had set out a score and was now tracing the notes of its melody. She worked thoughtfully at the unfamiliar tune, seemingly satisfied with herself or the piece I knew not which.

"That is a wistful tune Lady Mountfield," commented Julia.

"Do you like it dear?" It is the *Lacrimosa* from Mozart's Requiem – one of the pieces that I thought Rose might play at her recital."

"A recital, Lady Mountfield?"

"I think the girl is nearly ready for a public performance, don't you agree Edward? I was thinking of just a small gathering of my most intimate acquaintance."

"And what does Father think of this recital Mother?" I enquired.

"Oh, Edward darling, there is plenty of time for your father to alter his opinion," she replied.

I knew very well what my father would think of this little enterprise and the colourful language that would undoubtedly issue from his mouth on hearing of my mother's plans. Their disagreement would be avidly replayed and recounted in the servants' quarters no doubt, but I held my peace.

"When will the recital be held?" prompted the ever-solicitous Julia.

"Bless you dear, not until the Autumn, I thought it would be perfect to have a little soirée to coincide with the bringing in of the harvest. You know, just a few friends that we haven't seen since before the war, nothing too formal."

She at least had the good sense to be leaving a significant stretch of time for my father to become accustomed to her idea. That, I felt for all concerned, was one small mercy, but nevertheless I still suspected it would give ample scope for my father to rage and roar his disapproval whenever anyone was in earshot.

It was at this point that my father entered the drawing room. Barely pausing as he headed to pour himself a drink from the tray, he commanded my mother to cease playing. "Damn it woman, will you not stop that infernal racket, I swear I prefer that wretched girl's playing to yours. As I recall you used to be quite good. It must be as they say, we all lose proficiency in the things that we were once good at, do you not agree Julia?" he announced to my fiancée.

"You are gracious as always, darling, but I am merely seeing if this piece is suitable for Rose to play, not playing it myself, if you have a care to observe the difference." For once her comment was sharp, but as was the way of things between my parents, my father chose simply to ignore her.

"Now Edward," he continued, "you will know when it is that the schoolteacher will wed? As the landowner I think it only right I should send something."

In regard to this matter, I was one step ahead. "I have already arranged for a contribution to be made to the couple's celebrations, Father. Cook will be making some sundries for the wedding feast and I thought perhaps a barrel of ale for the men would go down well?"

"Oh yes, quite satisfactory. That will do nicely I think." Quickly changing tack he continued, "Well and what about this business of who is to be the new school teacher? I thought it would suit all concerned if this Mr Scrivens should be appointed to the position. Keep it in the family?"

"Is Miss Adam aware of the fact that she will lose her employ?" queried Julia.

"Why should she not be my dear? I'm sure that it will have been written into the woman's conditions of employment."

"Nevertheless, Sir Peter, it seems unjust, especially as her reputation as a teacher is exemplary," pressed Julia.

"But my dear, you are forgetting – a woman working after she is wed? That would be simply unthinkable, it would not be proper. Undeniably, it would be best if Mr Scrivens were to start at the earliest opportunity, even before the wedding takes place. That's if you think him a suitable candidate, Edward?" he deferred to me.

"He has, I'm sure Mother would agree, made a fine job of instructing some of the pupils..." I began; however, I was prevented from continuing.

"Certainly, certainly, well that's settled then. If the man can make a reasonable fist of teaching the village boys how to play the pianoforte, then there is no doubt he will make an excellent job of teaching the rest of them how to read and write. Teaching is teaching after all."

I was not sure whether the board would agree

with his conclusions, but I kept that sentiment to myself. Perhaps Mr Scrivens would prove himself to be an able teacher after all, but my father's mind was made up and of course he had the influence to see his preferences carried through.

"I will speak with Reverend Hawkins and acquaint him with your views Sir, for as you know he himself has had the duty of teaching the older boys of an afternoon," I conceded, saving the peace.

Despite my misgivings and after further investigation I was to discover that Mr Scrivens was indeed a qualified teacher, his other employ away from Long Wendon had made up the other portion of his salary whilst he had continued to work for Lady Mountfield and our little school one day a week. On Mondays he was Long Wendon School's piano master and for the rest of the week he had taught in an elementary school in North London. Quite how my mother had managed to persuade his other place of employ to release him for one day a week I do not know but persuaded they had been. My mother had once again surprised me.

CHAPTER 33

A WINTER WEDDING

William

Mr Scrivens took up the position of village schoolmaster in the parish of Long Wendon at the beginning of December. There was little more than three weeks of the school term left to run and I, for one, was not altogether happy with the change this brought to our school, for in comparison to Eliza Adam he was strict and sour, though I have to say not unfair in his approach. However, my main grievance against Mr Scrivens, an opinion shared by a good number of my peers, was the man's ability to make even the most enjoyable of topics unbelievably dull. How could this man at one moment inspire us with his love of music and at the next bring us so low with his colourless lessons in reading, writing and arithmetic?

Despite this change we somehow managed to keep our spirits cheerful, doubtless with the knowledge that the Christmas holiday would soon be upon us and of course there was the much-anticipated winter wedding to look forward to. The couple were to be married on

Boxing Day and I could not wait for the dancing, revelry and delights to begin for in my childish imagination I had magnified the event into something above the ordinary, a grand party that would be attended by the whole village.

Christmas day passed peacefully in our home, with only the customary visit to church to mark it out as different from any other day, saving a few choice victuals that my brother had somehow managed to lay by for the occasion. Instead of our usual work-day broth, there was beef and vegetables for the mid-day meal and for once my brother Tom had insisted on the preparation of it himself. In this one act my brother Tom proved himself to be contrary to the standard domestic practice of the time, for despite her tender age, my sister would have been expected to fulfil all the domestic chores around the house and especially on high days and holidays. For her part Rose had only to supply a plum pudding for dessert which was given to her by Mrs Stewart undoubtedly acting on an instruction from Lady Mountfield. Daniel Martin, making up the fourth in our small party, had brought a couple of jugs of ale as his contribution to our meal. He was still living in Long Wendon, having been kept on as a general handyman about the estate, but having secured a temporary lodging in the village he had at last moved out of our home which had felt very cramped with him in it. My brother had invited him to spend Christmas Day with us, on account of him having no family left in the village himself.

Boxing day dawned cold and clear and there was a good depth of snow under foot, so the village looked the perfect picture setting for a winter wedding. John and I and nearly half the other boys from the village who had managed to eschew family duties for the day had met on the common that morning to make ice houses and snow men and to have running snowball fights. I had brought a wrapper of bread and cheese as had my friend John, anticipating that we would stay well into the afternoon. It was only when the church bell chimed four and the daylight was almost gone that we ran back to our homes to warm ourselves by the hearth, strip ourselves of our now sodden clothes and to prepare to be the guards of honour for our former schoolmistress.

It was a little after six when we arrived at Long Wendon church. Dressed in our Sunday clothes and now joined by the rank and file of village girls, free at last from their daily chores, we filed into church to hear Eliza Adam and Mr Scrivens plight their troth each to the other. The church was packed with all manner of souls that evening, with the exception of the Mountfield family members who naturally would not attend in person. However, many of the household staff were among the numbered guests and there was much joy and celebration expressed by the congregation at large at the couple's union. The lean years of the war and its aftermath had not given much opportunity for celebration and it was as if this wedding gave all those who witnessed it a small reason to be joyful. If this seems a fanciful notion, believe me when I say that it was not. Perhaps it is best described in terms of a temporary release of knowing, of setting aside for a short while the knowledge of recent hardships and sufferings that the war had brought in its wake.

We children led the singing with an enthusiastic, though not always tuneful, rendition of *All Things Bright and Beautiful* which was Miss Adam's favourite children's hymn and at the close of the proceedings the whole congregation gave a spirited performance of *Abide with Me*. This last hymn was the cue for all the children to form a guard of honour outside the church door, and as you can imagine there was much excitable nudging and elbowing in our haste to perform this duty. Mr and Mrs Scrivens left the church and walked through an arch of holly and mistletoe.

Mr Scrivens, dressed in a rather worn single-breasted suit and tie of pre-war style looked older than his forty-one years and was as self-conscious as you would expect him to be, not being one to seek the limelight. His bride, in contrast, looked younger than her years, no-longer clothed in her customary school attire of high-necked blouse and long plain skirt, Eliza Adam was the epitome of the blushing bride dressed in a cream loose-fitting shift dress, ankle strap shoes and cream full-brimmed hat. She more than made up for the appearance of her somewhat dowdy bridegroom as she smiled and thanked each one of us in turn for our company while Mr Scrivens, his elbow linked through Eliza's, seconded his wife's thanks with a discreet but generous smile of his own. Perhaps after all, I reassured myself, Mr Scrivens was not such a bad match for Eliza Adam, though as my teacher he would always be the poorer in comparison to his wife.

The wedding feast was held in Long Wendon Village Hall which, when first constructed by the Mountfield family in the mid-1800s, had served first as a reading room for the community and later as a school before the current school building was erected at the turn of the century. It was a pretty stone-built hall, of an oddly square design which was uncommon for the period, with a high ceiling and high windows. The village women had turned out in force to decorate the hall that morning, such was the regard in which our former schoolmistress was held, that on entering there was not one corner of the room that had not been transformed by winter foliage comprising mainly of sprigs of holly and mistletoe. The hall smelt of candle wax, oranges (a grand treat provided by the grand family) and roasting meats, indeed the Mountfield family's generosity had ensured a fine dinner for the whole village to enjoy.

With the snow piled thick on the ground and the dark skies threatening a further fall, we quickly made our way across the lane, and on arrival we stamped the cloying snow from off our shoes and boots before entering into the warmth of the brightly lit hall. There was to be music and feasting and dancing that night and of course the liberal provision of meat and ale meant that the village men would be roundly satisfied. The music was a hotch-potch of country tunes played by village stalwarts such as Joseph Black who had played at every gathering I had ever attended in my short life, and I daresay at a great many more before I was born. The tunes were folk ditties handed down from father to son that were good dancing tunes but also the kind of music that invited any listener of good voice to join in with gusto.

It was not long before all those who were able to dance were up on the floor, myself included, and I'm sure my friend John and I made a right exhibition of ourselves, though not so much as those who had taken rather more of the

Mountfield's ale than they ought.

I sat perched on a bench near the door when Rose, flushed from her own turns on the dance floor came towards me and took my hand in hers. She wore an old dress that had been our mother's which she had diligently spent the last month taking in at the waist and up at the hem in order that she might have something pretty to wear at the wedding dance. The overall effect was well done, though her needlework could not match my mother's, but that said she looked a picture with her rich black hair tied back, her cheeks pinkly flushed and her eyes sparkling with delight.

"Dance with me Billy," she coaxed as she pulled me to my feet. "Tom won't dance with anyone, not even his own sister, and Hetty Spencer is dancing with Arthur Pollock, so I've no partner."

Of course, I would dance with her, her joy was infectious, and although she was a girl, she was also my sister, so I figured that that didn't really count. I felt confident there would be no follow-up smirking from my classmates when we all returned to school for the new term.

She pulled me quickly into the centre of the room, the music carrying me along in her wake as we skipped and hopped and turned about amidst the throng of village folk young and old who had assembled to enjoy the pleasure of the dance. My cheeks began to redden again with the exertion, but my sister's warmth of spirit kept me on my feet as up and down the dance floor we travelled for four or more tunes. Each song was interspersed with summary clapping from the dancers and onlookers and as we were about to embark upon yet another set, I felt the floor disappear beneath my feet as I was unceremoniously lifted aside and shoved towards the refreshment table by none other than Daniel Martin. "Move aside Billy and take some water why don't you, for your face is as red as a beet and you look all out of puff." This was accompanied by a smattering of laughter from those nearby who had seen me so efficiently man-handled out of the way, in order that the young man could take a turn with my sister.

"Now Rose, you shouldn't be dancing with your little brother all this time, when there's a man who's willing and able to step in time with you. Men are scarce on the ground and I dare say I'm something of a prize as a dancing partner!" he continued holding my sister fast by the hand and placing the other in the small of her back as the music began again in earnest.

There was merriment for certain in my sister's eyes as she lifted her chin up to face him. "And what prize are you Dan Martin to any girl?" she chided. "For I've seen you dancing and you've two left feet for sure. You stepped on Bessy's heel for she showed me how it had reddened up so cruelly."

"What do I care for your friend's heel? I swear it was no fault of mine, if the silly girl had not danced like a skittering lamb in a field, she would still be dancing now, for her legs were going in all directions and how was I to avoid treading on her foot?" he returned.

"Daniel Martin, you should not say so," she chided.

"And why not if it's the truth and no lie. I had much better dance with you pretty Rose, though you are as young and foolish as any girl I've known."

My sister's cheeks blushed pinker at his words, as he steered her across the dance floor.

From the corner of my eye, I saw my brother Tom watching them intently, but his face showed none of the distaste that I was feeling on my sister's behalf. I do not know what it was that cautioned me against the man, for I had nothing to confirm my distrust of him, but I did not like the arrogance with which he appraised my sister, as if she were already his to own and to do with as he pleased. Rose was little more than the child I still was myself and this man was too rooted in the adult world for me to feel at ease with how he looked on her.

My brother Tom smiled as they passed him

by, taking only delight in the sight of his sister and his friend dancing together. I could not fathom his reaction, but then after all, perhaps prejudiced by my own childish hatred of his brother, I was mistaken in my distrust of Daniel Martin.

A little over an hour into the celebrations Edward Mountfield, accompanied by Lady Julia and Edwards's brother Arthur joined the festivities, come to bestow their congratulations in person on the happy couple. A silence fell over the dancing as they entered the hall as the musicians briefly suspended their playing, but Edward swiftly motioned for them to continue and so the dancing very quickly resumed.

Arthur, whom we had not seen in the county of late, looked older, but perhaps no wiser for his time served in the army. His boyish good looks, etched on the collective memory of the villagers prior to his departure to the front had now resolved themselves into a very handsome set of more mature features; firm jaw, straight nose in fact so closely resembling the likeness of his older brother Peter that Abe Holden, having imbibed a bit too much of the ale supplied by the great family, proclaimed out loud that it was the young master risen from the dead. The resumption of the band mercifully drowned out the old man's protestations and Arthur himself, his eye filled with merriment, seemed to find the incident amusing and not in the least bit distasteful or impertinent.

Arthur was certainly a gallant addition to the gathering, sweeping up Lady Julia and pulling her into the middle of the dancing, a gesture which was applauded by the majority of party goers. Edward, however, could not help feeling that his father would be apoplectic at the thought of his youngest son and eldest son's fiancée mixing so publicly with the common village celebrants.

My brother Tom brought up a chair for Edward and sat with him, being one of only a few persons in the room not dancing himself.

"Tom, will you not join the dancing?" remarked Edward, with one eye following his brother and Julia's progress across the floor?

"No Sir. I make a poor partner; I've never took to the dancing."

"Nonsense man, go and do your duty, for young men are few on the ground, and I'm sure any young woman would rather have her foot stepped upon, than have no dance partner at all."

Tom, of course could not refuse the command of Edward Mountfield and reluctantly escorted Bessy Trent onto the floor where he promptly stepped on the girl's other heel.

Edward caught my eye observing him. "He

wasn't underestimating his abilities when he described them as poor," he confided as he laughed at my brother's efforts. I smiled back conspiratorially. "Your sister, however…" he continued, diverted by the sight of Rose gracefully being led around the floor by Daniel Martin, "has a very light step, certainly a joy to behold."

He turned his attention back to me. "Now why don't you run along and get some of that good food inside you, for it certainly looks a veritable feast?" The implication was that I continued to look underfed, which of course I was. He turned his eyes back to my sister and I briefly watched him, watching her, the smile still on his face.

Quickly, however, my stomach directed me towards the table that was heaped with all manner of delicious looking fare.

CHAPTER 34

SNOW

Tom

I go outside to catch my breath, fair put out I've had to dance with nearly half the village girls, though I know I've served them all ill, for I am no dancer. But how could I say against the master when he urged me to it? More fool they, for putting up with my stray feet. I was sure to do them injury, yet they would dance with me.

I look up and see there's clouds in the sky. It's a chill wind and I know there'll be snow falling this night. I reckon we'd best get back afore it comes down, so I turn to fetch Rose and Billy when I hear voices from behind the hall. The talk is none so friendly.

Before I can go and see what's doing, my sister Rose comes into sight. She looks backwards as she runs so she don't see me. "I never will!" she shouts.

"Rose, wait up there." I grab a hold of her wrist as she passes. "What's amiss girl?"

She scowls at me, a look of pure temper on her. "Nothing," she says, and she looks at her shoes. I see her face is red and her hair's come out of her braid.

Next comes my friend Dan. "Nothing is it?" he laughs.

"What's amiss?" I ask again.

"Nothing Tom, nothing to get you all riled up I swear." His eyes are sparking, and I know that look in my friend – I know 'tis fun is all, not spite.

"Nothing, save that I tried to steal a kiss from your pretty sister. Where's the harm, I say? You know I've taken a liking to her, though she's young and I maybe should have waited a year. But I reckon she knows now I'm set on her and I'm sorry pretty Rose to have frighted you, though truest word I meant no harm." He raises his hands as he talks, like he's trying to make amends for that stolen kiss. He sways a bit, and I can see that he's none too steady on his feet.

"Dan, what were you about? It's certain my sister's startled for she's but fourteen." Though, in truth I'm not mad at Dan for saying his piece, though my sister's so young. It's all I can do to keep my face buttoned down from laughing at Rose who has her fists tight as can be and her face is streaked as red as a beet, she's in so much of a temper. Instead, I take my friend's part and try to make her see there's no matter here. "Rose, don't take on so, Dan says he means no harm and I know his word is true more than most anyone hereabouts. For my sake, will you not make up and us all be friends again?"

Dan stands there yet, swaying and grinning like a cat and it's plain he's had too much ale for sure and maybe that's what's talking in him. I know too our Rose will not back down, for she's all in a stir.

"When you're all grown Rose, I'll wed you. See, I'll draw a cross on my heart."

In truth or no my fool friend draws the same across his chest and I see the fire in Rose's eyes flare right back up.

"I won't marry you, never!"

I'm taken aback by the strength of her passion. "Hush now Rose, Dan's a good man, no need to fuss against him." Before I can say more and before Rose can turn away Dan reaches for her hand and kisses it on the back like she's some kind of lady.

Rose is in a boiling rage now and I'm rare bursting to laugh at Dan for acting like some fool lord and master in kissing my sister's fingers, but instead I say to Rose as stern as I can, "Go and fetch Billy and tell him we're away home."

She turns and marches back into the hall without a word and now I can't keep from letting out my laughter. I should be angry at my friend but instead I clap Dan on the shoulder. "Go home and sleep it off."

"Sorry," he slurs. "Tell the girl I'm sorry."

"You'll tell her yourself tomorrow. Go home."

My friend sways along the path, back towards the church and round the corner and out of sight. I scratch my head; I've never known Dan get so drunk before on so little drink. When I think on it, I reckon a match between my friend and my sister would be a fine thing. Better a match than she's a right to, I reckon. I can't figure why she took so bad with the idea, she seemed taken with him when they was dancing.

Rose and Billy and I walk up the lane in silence. I send Billy on ahead when we're close by the cottage, saying we'll catch up. Rose walks sullenly beside me, all joy gone from the day, she kicks the snow as she goes along. "Your shoes'll be soaked through."

"Our mum would say that," she accuses.

"I don't want to fight Rose."

"I don't like him," she says.

"How can you not? He's my friend."

"He's your friend not mine."

I pull her up short and we stand facing each other. The sky is real threatening now and the first flakes have started to fall. "I know Daniel, he's not one to say something he don't mean. I think he has a liking for you." She stays tight-lipped, arms folded hard across her chest.

"Listen to me. He shouldn't have tried to kiss you, but he meant no harm by it. Don't take against him for that, take a time to think about it a while longer and you might change your mind."

"He scared me," she says and now it's me that's doing all the talking when it's usually Rose who has all the words. I wipe my hand across my eyes and I see in hers the child she still is.

"Tis nothing to be scared of in Dan. He had a drink in him, is all. Next time you see him he'll be like a church mouse, you'll see."

"I don't want to marry him; I don't want to marry anyone!" she shouts at me, and I know she's in earnest. "I told you and you think I don't know my own mind, but I do. I want to be a teacher and I can be, I can be Tom if you'll only let me."

I'm angry at her now, but I bite my tongue on it. "You'll do as I say, Rose. I'll not make you wed a man if your heart's set against it, whether it be Dan or any man, but I think you a fool to not think on't some more, that's if he'll look at you now after what you said to him. Daniel Martin is a good man, but you won't see it being as your head's so stuffed full of that teacher's fancy ideas, but it ends now. Do you hear? You'll not go back to school; you'll go out to work as you should have done this year past. Now get on home."

There are tears in her eyes, but she doesn't say a word, just turns and runs after Billy.

CHAPTER 35

IN SERVICE

Edward

After the wedding, a fortnight passed before I set eyes on Rose again. It had been a little over a week since her circumstances had changed and I was seated in the far corner of the drawing room, half perusing an article in the Times Newspaper. The light had grown dim, and I was feeling the strain in my one good eye. I had determined to put the paper aside and seek out Julia's company when the girl entered the room. She did not immediately note my presence and so I watched, curious to see if her new position had improved or diminished her.

She was wearing the uniform of a maid, polished black shoes, ankle length black skirt, faded and shiny in patches from wear, a white blouse, and tied around her waist, a lace-fringed apron, which I noted was none too clean. The clothes had clearly had a previous owner: shapeless and loose-fitting on her lean frame. Her face was scrubbed clean, her hair tied back untidily with a black bow, with just a few strands of her lovely tresses falling free to frame her face. That face was a little pale, her two cheeks pinked with exertion, but there was yet a spark in her pure dark eyes for all her obvious fatigue. Under her arm she carried a pile of musical scores which she put lightly down on top of the piano. With a quick step she crossed towards the fire that was struggling for life in the grate, knelt and began to pile extra coals on top, using the poker to kindle it back to flame. Next, she put down the poker and stretched out her hands to warm them.

"Are you cold?"

Startled she spun round sharply and was on her feet in one swift movement. "Begging your pardon Sir, I didn't…"

I stopped her with a motion of my hand. "Rose you look all done in, bring up that chair to the fire and sit awhile."

"Sir?"

"Please do as I say, Rose." It was a command and though most certainly ill at ease with my request she complied: she pulled one of the armchairs a little closer to the fire and waited for me to take my place in the other before sinking down into hers. Her eyes did not look away this time, but gazed upon my own, her chin raised.

"I'm glad your spirits seem unbowed," I observed drily. She continued to hold my gaze, provoking a smile from my lips.

"I did not see you Sir."

"Clearly you did not, otherwise you would not have stoked up the fire and wasted my mother's coals merely to warm your servant's bones," I teased.

She blanched a little, but pleasingly held her nerve. "I had instructions to see to the fire Sir," she countered.

"Well said!" This time I laughed out loud. "And how do you find life in service child? Speak truthfully, for I will know if you tell me a lie," I commanded.

"It is very good of Lady Mountfield to find me a position Sir."

"Damn and blast my mother, I don't care a jot about my mother's benevolence. Now answer my question truthfully."

"I can manage the work, but I'd much rather be in school." With these words her eyes flickered down to her hands clasped in her lap.

"There you see, was that so hard? Honesty at last."

Instantly her eyes had returned to face mine.

"I am a servant Sir. I cannot say otherwise than that I am grateful."

There it was: the bite, the spark, the flash of spirit that so fascinated and invited me. Yet again her words had given me pause. I had provoked her response and curiously it had made me ashamed in some small part, for had she not spoken the entire truth just as I had commanded her? What else should she have felt but gratitude, there were many in her position who would have been glad of the work and the wage. But not Rose, Rose desired more.

"I am teasing you child," I said.

She continued to look at me, knowing full well that she had spoken out of turn.

"This conversation will go no further than between ourselves Rose. Are you still set on this notion of yours: of becoming a schoolteacher child?"

She looked at me, as if she were thinking of the precise wording to her answer. Cautiously she continued, "Sir, more than anything. But 'tis impossible, my brother will not allow it." Such was the passion aroused in her, that I swear that I saw tears in her eyes.

"What has your brother against the idea?"

"He says our folk have always been servants and labourers. That it's not for us, not for me to think of bettering myself. What's good enough for him is good enough for us all."

"Your father had a skill did he not?"

"He was a cobbler Sir," she stammered clearly disconcerted by mention of her father, fearing no doubt that I would rebuke her for his disgrace.

"Yes, I see." I looked further into her dark black eyes, so full of passionate hopes that were on the very precipice of being snuffed out. All innocence lost as child turned to girl turned to woman and the reality of her circumstances would inexorably break her dreams. It was indeed a fanciful analogy that I chided myself with. Surely it was not my responsibility to raise her up, it was not I who had laid her low, it was not I who through my actions on the field of war had wrought shame and stigma to bear on her and all her kin? So why did I care? What drove me to care?

"What of your schooling girl?" I continued sharply. "You attended the village elementary school, a year longer than most I hear. Should you not have rather attended the secondary, if this was your ambition?" I rebuked. "I am correct that you would need a clutch of examination certificates behind you if you wished to gain access to a training establishment for teachers?"

She kept my gaze, her chin lifted. "I was a monitor and helped with the other children and

Miss Adam was teaching me harder work Sir."

It was clear that Miss Adam's encouragement of the girl's dreams could only extend so far. And how could it be otherwise? How did an orphaned child, such as Rose, find the spirit let alone the means to raise herself above her situation when cold reality dictated that one labourer's wage was the mainstay to feed and clothe the three of them? The child's dream was no more than that, just a fantasy that her birthright would always deny her. Assuredly I was comfortable from my viewpoint of the way the world was. There were the landowners and the lords, the rich, my class, my forbears and then there was everyone else – the ranked masses of the poor far below us whose needs must grind out their daily bread. It was simply the way of things, but yet why then did it trouble me so, for surely it did, that this girl for want of coin and position could not reach above herself.

I shook my head. "Let me think on this dilemma of yours Rose, but be clear on this, I promise nothing more than that I will give your situation further thought."

"Sir. Why Sir?"

Why indeed? Perhaps the simple truth of it was that I was coming to realise my mother's guileless act of benevolence towards Rose had had unforeseen consequences. She has lifted her out of the common way of things, and that unlooked for act of kindness had proved to be prophetic. That act had fed the girl's own fancies and dreams, and those dreams, day following day, were nurtured by her own unquestionable skill.

"I do not like to see talent wasted," I answered gruffly. The answer would serve for the moment. "Now come Rose, if you are warmed enough from the fire, perhaps you should begin your practice, for is that not why you are in the drawing room?"

"Yes Sir, I've to practice two hours every day after my work."

"On top of your duties?"

She acknowledged my question with a curt not of her head, then sprang from her perch and readied herself at the piano. I stayed seated by the fire letting the sweet music lift my own spirits, closing my eyes as I reflected more upon the girl's circumstances, wondering all the while how I had come to care so deeply for the fate of this orphaned girl.

CHAPTER 36

LIKE MOTHS TO A FLAME

Edward

Though the light was fading, the curtains had not yet been drawn. I had dismissed the servant who had come into the drawing room moments before for that express purpose. The day had been sharp cold, but clear and I wanted to see the last embers of the day as the sun began to sink behind the distant tree-line. I stood with my cane at the verandah windows and watched as Mr Frances, Tom Baxter and the new man Daniel Martin walked past the ornamental pond at the end of the long lawn.

At length the lad Billy came running up and the old man paused to ruffle his hair before the group turned away and headed towards the back of the house. They paused a little way off, perhaps to listen to Rose's studied playing, for though the fire was lit, and the day had been chilled I had insisted on a window being left open. With the house shut up for the Winter, all hatches battened down, the air could become stale and cloying, so I insisted that at the very least the rooms that I would occupy should be aired during the daylight hours.

At length I crossed to the window and latched it shut, then awkwardly began to draw the curtains. All the while the girl continued to play and play well, though I could see that though her fingers were still nimble across the keys her general disposition was one of weariness.

As I returned to the fireside to resume my seat my mother, Arthur and Julia entered the drawing room.

"We have come to hear the urchling!" pronounced my brother as he headed towards the drink's cabinet.

"Arthur, darling, the girl is no such thing as you very well know," admonished my mother. "Well, well, no matter, you must think her much improved?"

"I have to hand it to you Mother, your protégé can certainly play, though I must say if you are to furnish her with employment as well as financing her musical talent, as I see you have judging by her attire, you might have dressed her in clothes that actually fit. I'm sure father will have a conniption when he sees her. Care to join me in a pre-prandial drink brother?" he asked holding the decanter aloft.

"Pour me a whiskey Arthur and for goodness'

sake stop embarrassing the girl for something that's not her fault."

"Well said Edward," interjected Julia, coming as I knew she would to Rose's defence. "I'm sure Lady Mountfield has ordered Rose a proper uniform and her present dress is only a temporary measure."

"Certainly Julia, you sweet, kind girl, new clothes have been ordered, but these things take time. Now Rose, child, how are you getting on with the *Lacrimosa*?"

Rose finished the phrase she was playing, slowly lifted her fingers from the keys and with a small smile turned on the seat to face her benefactress. "I love to play it ma'am for 'tis a lovely piece – though there are some difficult parts for my fingers to get round ma'am." Her face was pale through tiredness, though her eyes still shone at the thought of the music.

"Gracious, Rose you look positively ill child. Are you sick?"

"No ma'am."

"Not sick mother, just all done in by the look of it. What did you expect? She starts her work before the crack of dawn, do you not pretty Rose?" commented Arthur, but did not wait for a reply. "Next, she is here near 'til supper time at your insistence and then I expect she must go home to her hovel and fetch and carry again for that morose brother of hers and the mute boy."

Julia was swift to lessen the girl's discomfort. "We would very much like to hear you play the piece and then perhaps Lady Mountfield will excuse you early?" This last was addressed to my mother who of course acceded to Julia's request.

The music began, slow and haunting, filling the air with its melancholy, hushing the gathered company to silence. It was not faultless, but it was indeed a beautiful piece. Rose's hands fell still at last.

"Very good, very good indeed. I am much contented with your progress, child," fussed my mother. "Now run along as dear Julia suggests, for the night I fear is already drawing in."

She gathered together the music, curtsied and left.

"What an odd little thing she is," exhaled my brother as the door clicked gently shut.

"Her duties will of course have an effect on her ability to practice properly mother," I remarked lazily. "Perhaps it is time for your generosity to be diverted towards another worthy recipient?" I continued.

I admit that at the time I felt that I was manipulating my mother, and in truth I was uncomfortable at employing such a tactic for such an action smacked of the parent who owned the least of my affection – my father.

"No by all means!" cried my mother. "What of the recital Edward? I will not countenance it. You have heard the child on many an occasion, you of all people must recognise her skill and see that she is most worthy of this attention. Her duties will simply have to be curtailed in order that she is able to practice."

"What, pay her wages so that she can play the pianoforte? That's preposterous Mother, Father really will have a fit." observed Arthur drily.

"I think Lady Mountfield is simply suggesting that her hours be somewhat reduced, for it is for Lady Mountfield's recital that the girl needs to practice and not merely for her own betterment."

"Oh Julia, thank you, I despair of my sons sometimes, I really do. You are the most sensible one amongst us. Now I must go at once and speak to the housekeeper about changing Rose's duties." And with that she swept from the room.

"Well bless me Julia, you would put Lloyd George to shame with your diplomacy," Arthur rounded on Julia with mirth in his eyes as the door once again clicked shut.

Arthur topped up his glass, filled a second one and handed it to Julia. We sat nursing our own thoughts for a short time until at length my brother returned to me, his demeanour serious for once, his usual levity muted. "Now brother, you must advise me. Father demands that I consider my future."

"In what way? Does he mean that you should go up to Oxford?"

He waved this aside. "No, no I am done with all that, but the confounded thing is I haven't the deuced idea what to do. Father says that our class should set an example, that the landed gentry should no longer be idle, but that we should lead by example which is pretty rich coming from him don't you think? The thing is Edward, I had thought I might like to try my hand at running the estate, but you seem to be doing a damn fine job of it without my help, so I'll just have to find something else to do with my time. I had thought that being a clergyman wouldn't be so bad, but…"

"You a clergyman!" I snorted. This I felt keenly would be the very last occupation that my youngest brother should consider.

"Edward, it's a perfectly fine career for a young man," interjected Julia.

"No, it isn't, well I mean yes, of course it is, but not for my brother and Arthur knows it, he is just jesting with us," I replied.

"Well, well I suppose you're right."

"Of course, I am right!"

"Why?" Julia asked.

"Well for one thing I don't believe in God," replied my brother, fully aware of the reaction that this statement would provoke in my fiancée.

"Arthur really, don't for goodness' sake let Mother hear you saying that." I turned next to Julia with a few conciliatory words. "He doesn't mean it Julia; he's merely being controversial."

"Controversial? Well, I daresay you're right but I'm damned if I don't mean it. The war has knocked God out of better men than me wouldn't you agree brother?"

"Arthur!" I brought him up sharply. "This is neither the time nor the place."

"Edward? Well, I suppose so," he acquiesced. "You are quite right of course, brother mine, we must never bring up the wretched subject with ladies present. Either way, I'm certain of one thing, I don't have the disposition to bring out goodness and devotion in others when in myself I find those qualities seriously lacking."

"What about the law?" asked Julia, seeking to steer the subject away from its current course.

"Dear me no! Simply preposterous idea, Julia – too much book-learning and ultimately too damned depressing."

We spent the next half hour or so debating the merits of numerous professions without my brother considering any of our suggestions with much enthusiasm, save perhaps a slight leaning towards a career in politics. In the end Arthur was brought round to the opinion that perhaps after all he had better go up to Oxford as an intermediate step which would at any rate placate our father, and which would more importantly give my brother a justifiable reason to delay any decisions about his future for a year or two at the very least.

At length our conversation returned to the subject of my mother's protégé, giving Arthur the excuse to ponder the circumstances of another over having to dwell any longer upon his own.

"And how is the girl to achieve such an ambition?" queried Arthur. "Surely it will take more than a labourer's wages to get her the education she will need, and I can't see that homespun of a brother of hers putting himself out to help her."

"I think you do the man a dis-service Arthur," cautioned Julia. "Certainly, he does not support her ambition at present as he assumes that there is no way that she can be supported in it. He is the sole keeper of his brother and sister and must feel his burden keenly."

"But if the monetary burden of the enterprise were lifted, you think the man would change his mind?" Arthur considered.

"Perhaps," I interjected. "But there is also her secondary education to consider. The girl says that her former schoolteacher tutored her after the conclusion of the school day, but due to her recent change in circumstance she is no longer at school."

"Mother could easily be persuaded to support the girl through any training. Father would have a fit of course which would make the enterprise all the sweeter," commented Arthur gleefully. "Do you think that Mrs Scrivens, now that she is no longer the village schoolteacher, would welcome the chance to further her star pupil's ambition, for was it not she who put this notion into the girl's head in the first place?"

"Yes, so Rose has averred," confirmed Julia.

"Well then, it is settled. All we need to do is convince Mother to open her purse strings and to persuade the Scrivens woman to educate her, which will mean," enthused my brother, "that the girl's duties as a maid must be further reduced so that she can fit in her studies, which of course will mean that Father will doubtless disapprove. What a delicious conspiracy we are hatching – you may count me in!"

It was not what my father's reaction would be that concerned me, but rather Tom Baxter's. For all that I had observed of the man, he was proud and upright and would if we were not careful regard the whole enterprise as charity. Though born to different worlds I was coming to realise that his sense of dignity and duty, learned as a common soldier, was no less worthy of respect than my own keen sense of those emotions. I did not want my mother to ride rough-shod over this man's obligation to his sister: this venture I concluded must be tackled with the lightest of touches. The seed must be slowly planted and steadily nurtured and I would need to borrow some of my fiancée's skills of diplomacy to achieve it, while at the same time reigning in my mother's and now my brother's enthusiasm for a quick resolution to our plans.

In the end it took a little over a two month to clear the way with all parties, before Rose herself was informed of our proposal, and even at that I feared it was too swift a resolution to salve the sensibilities of her brother, but what could I do? My sole purpose was to further the ambitions of the girl and I would use my position, such as it was, to achieve that end.

CHAPTER 37

A PRETTY TUNE

William

As I rounded the west end of the house I saw Tom, Mr Frances and Daniel Martin making their way towards the furthest edge of the pond. They seemed to be in close conversation, tools in hand from their day's labour and did not notice my approach until I was nearly upon them.

Mr Frances reached out his hand and touched the top of my head in an act of affectionate greeting. "Well now Billy, I see you've been after visiting Mrs Stewart from the way you've come round."

I smiled and nodded my head, my belly full on account of Mrs Stewart's kindness.

"You'll not be wanting any supper at home then?" asked my brother raising an eyebrow.

"Nonsense lad, his belly'll be rumbling before he's got halfway back and no mistake."

"I reckon you've the right of it there Mr

Frances, the boy's nowt but bones," chipped in Dan Martin, extracting a tight laugh from my brother and a full rounded one from the old gardener.

The old man's gaze turned from us towards the house and verandah as the light evening breeze carried the sound of music through the open window.

"Bless me, but your sister's a fine player Tom, for it must be herself who's playing. I know the mistress is a grand player herself, but I reckon your sister's got the better touch."

All this elicited from Tom was a short grunt, but he joined us in our silence nonetheless, as much enraptured by the sweet tune as were we all.

"Tis a rare talent for certain she has." Mr Frances broke our reverie at last.

"But to what end is what I want to know," mused Tom, more to himself than to any of the present company.

"If Mr Hawkins asked her to play at church every Sunday, he'd be sure to fill up his congregation."

"Why Daniel Martin, you are a wicked fellow for saying so." Mr Frances turned to my brother's friend but with mirth in his eyes. "Reverend Hawkins can more than fill up his church of a Sunday, though I own you he's a fire and brimstone reverend. Why he surely puts the fear of God into my old bones."

"You, Mr Frances? You're a true and honest man, ain't he Tom? You've nothing to fear from his churching."

"My Bess, God rest her soul, used to say that he was the kind of reverend as made you believe you were sinful even if you weren't."

"So, Rose would be doing us all a good turn by making the Reverend's sermons sweeter by her music."

"You do him wrong, Dan, to mock him, for he's a good, kind man and took Billy and Rose in when no-one else would, and I'll not forget it in a hurry."

"That's right, God's truth it is lad," replied Mr Frances. "We were just having our fun, but I reckon you know first-hand of that man's kindness. Still your sister plays a pretty tune and a sweet one and t'would do a power of good to them that heard her, my own poor soul included rather than just the odd snatch or two like now."

We listened a while longer until at length I saw the young master stand and cross stiffly to the window. He latched it shut and pulled the curtain across, locking my sister's music in and we listeners out.

CHAPTER 38

A PROPOSITION

William

The winter cold lingered until the end of January to be replaced swiftly by the early onset of Spring – a month of mild, dry days and February sunshine. As February turned into March the weather seemed to follow the fortunes of the nation. The immediate post-war period injected a temporary boost to the working man, but it was to be short-lived. Further into the decade and the levels of unemployment would rise beyond all expectation, depressing the workforce and plunging the country into a period of industrial unrest. But we were not there yet, the changeable weather pattern of March 1920 led to a dull and wet April and spirits in this small corner of the land were dampened, but not yet dimmed.

My sister Rose had been in service for nearly three months, and I had observed, in this brief time, a change in her. When first she began her duties at Grange Park, she had come home wearied from the long days, her nature burdened not by the work, but more by what that employment signified. Where once she had greeted all her trials, tribulations and hardships with fierceness and a determined spirit to overcome, her mood was now subdued. Rose could now see her life stretching ahead of her, the daily grind of duty and service that would continue until she would one day marry, that grind only to be replaced by yet another drudgery and a new set of duties and responsibilities. Every day as I came to meet my sister after her piano practice and we would walk back together across the fields to the cottage, I would note how she had become just a little less joyful, a little less light of heart, a little less like the sister I loved until one glorious, extraordinary day.

The date of Monday April fifth is indelibly printed on my memory as the day my sister's crushed spirits were revived and all her pent-up happiness returned treble-fold. It was the day that Edward Mountfield's plan was realised.

Her joy was infectious, instantaneous as she ran from the open verandah doors. I stared with astonishment as I watched my brother Tom emerge slowly from the drawing room with Edward Mountfield. They exchanged a few brief words and solemnly the master's son shook my brother's hand and turned back towards the house. Tom stared at his hand as if it were some kind of alien appendage, a curious bafflement cast across his face, the bewildered soldier standing in no-man's land not knowing how he had come to be there.

I had scarcely witnessed this curious exchange when my sister caught me up in her arms and whirled me round and round, squeezing the very breath from me. Her eyes glistened, and though I could see she was fair tired out from her day's labours, the sheer force of her delight kept me aloft and twirling until Tom caught up to us both and set me on my feet again.

"Oh, Billy, Billy, you'll never guess what's happened," she exclaimed. "It's true, it's true, I swear. I am to be a teacher after all and Lady Mountfield and Mr Edward and even Mrs Scrivens, who is Miss Adam as you know, are all to help me to it and…"

"Hush girl, where's your sense? Your brother knows full well who Mrs Scrivens is," interrupted my brother.

"I know, I know he does, but I'm that made up by it. Tom, thank you, thank you, for I know how you was against it but it's what I want, and you don't really mind, do you Tom?"

He held my sister at arms' length by her shoulders. "Settle down, won't you Rose."

She looked solemnly into his eyes. "You really don't mind?"

He scratched his head and with a quiet look of resignation on his face he answered. "It don't look like I've a right to mind, seeing as I'm not paying for it girl, now do it?"

This then was the plain reality; what could my brother do? Even if he had been amenable to Rose's wish to become a teacher and supported wholeheartedly her pursuit of that ambition, he had not the means to do it. Tom I knew to be a proud man and what of that? It must have troubled that pride greatly to stand there, cap in hand before the master knowing that this further act of charity to our sister was but one more thing he would feel himself beholden for.

There was silence between them, just for a moment, and then my brother's look softened towards her. He dropped his hands from her shoulders and with his right ran his fingers through his hair. "'Tis truly what you want?"

"More than anything in the world!" she gushed.

"Rose now don't start talking all foolish, like. I reckon it is what it is. Bless me, a teacher is it, my own sister's to be a teacher?" These words were spoken more to himself than to my sister and me. He put his arm around Rose's shoulder, a rare show of affection towards her, and we started to walk. "Let's get on home and you can tell Billy all about it once we've had our supper, for I reckon the boy'll be wanting a bit to eat though he's already visited Mrs Stewart's kitchen not long since." With this he raised an eyebrow to me, and I returned his almost smile.

For once our evening was one filled with warmth and good humour. Shutting the door on the dark of night that had advanced so quickly behind us as we made our way home, my brother quickly set to making up the fire. Rose busied herself clearing the breakfast dishes that in our haste we had left sitting that morning as my brother and I had headed out to work and school respectively. It was usual for my sister to leave before us, on account of her early starts at Grange Park, but still she would be expected to cook and clean, though her hours out of the cottage were in truth much longer than mine or my brother's. But today, all care of this labour was forgotten as she set about her tasks and prepared our supper.

"I've not to start 'til eight from now on Billy," Rose continued the chatter that had bubbled out of her ever since she had announced her news. "And that'll be ever so much better for it means I can get supper started afore I leave and not have so much to do when I'm back. Now there'll be no reason for Tom to growl and grumble when there's no food on the table and he says he's fair starving of hunger and…"

"I don't growl…" Tom tried to interrupt, but Rose's gabble would not be stopped.

"You do so too, Tom! But now you'll have no need is all I say for everything's going to be better. Mrs Scrivens is going to teach me in the afternoons and I'm still to do the piano practice for the mistress, and, and, and…"

And assuredly there was to be no stopping of my sister's 'ands' that night for she was wrapped up so tight in her own small world of happiness that there was no-one who could dampen her joy and none there that would want to. Tom's mood for once was light, caught up by the whirlwind of youthful hope and delight that was my sister and we all three went to bed that night content at least for that brief moment with the lives that fate had dealt us.

CHAPTER 39

A SECOND PROPOSITION

Edward

Mrs Scrivens came at two o'clock on a Monday, Wednesday and Thursday afternoon for the expressed purpose of preparing Rose to sit the examinations she would need to apply to teacher training college. It was agreed between my mother and the former schoolteacher that this would be more than adequate to achieve the desired results for the girl, considering her current age and the fact that she would not be eligible to apply to such an institution until she turned eighteen.

The lessons could well have been accommodated in one of the rooms off the servants' hall, but I had convinced my mother that they would be in no-one's way if instead the drawing room were used for the purpose. I reasoned that there would be far fewer distractions as the room was only ever used by myself in the afternoons as a place to sit and read once I had dealt with the business of running the estate. Julia likewise would often gravitate there, expressing the view that she found the light favourable and the room itself comfortable and less formal than other parts of the house. But I suspected, as was the case for myself, that it was the girl that attracted her. We had formed a new alliance by our vested interest in her education and, like the idle creatures we were, we were keen to see how this enterprise would progress. Today, however, I was on my own. My fiancée had gone to visit an old acquaintance who had just moved into the county and was not expected back until later that day.

Mrs Scrivens and Rose sat at a little table placed on the opposite side of the room, close by the verandah window to catch the best of the natural light. An atlas lay open between them and so I surmised it must be a geography lesson that they were engaged in. The girl was clearly engrossed and animated in the subject, and I observed there was much light chatter between them, Mrs Scrivens exercising a sisterly affection for her pupil. At last, the book was closed, and the former schoolmistress started to pack her things away.

"Well Rose that will do for today I think but, if you can find the time, please read the next chapter of your book."

"Thank you, Mrs Scrivens."

She smiled at the girl and patted her arm.

"I will see you on Wednesday. Good day, Mr Mountfield."

I waited to hear the soft click of the door shutting. Rose meanwhile tidied her books into a neat pile and stacked them on the shelf behind the piano, retrieving her music scores as she did so.

"Lady Mountfield is indisposed with a headache and will not be down to hear you play Rose, but I will stay while you practice."

"Yes Sir," she replied and quickly began to set up her music sheets on the stand.

"Wait, there is no need to rush to begin," I admonished. "Come and sit by the fire and tell me about your studies."

Her quick mind questioned my command but she readily acquiesced, stepped towards the fire and heeding my impatient gesture to be seated, took the chair opposite mine. I thought for a moment that she would curl up her legs underneath her, cat-like, but she did not. "Sir, you've been here this whole time…" She bit her lip and I smiled.

"And should know full well what you have been studying," I finished her impertinence for her.

She had the grace to a least appear chagrined and pretend to be absorbed for some moments with picking at a thread on her dress. But she was not bowed, and I caught the thrill of it.

I cocked my head towards her. "What do you want to ask?" I challenged her to continue. She eyed me cautiously her curiosity warring all the while with her knowledge that we walked once again upon dangerous ground. Acutely aware of the inequality in our positions, maid and master, master and maid I silently willed her to meet my challenge.

"Lady Julia..." she began, still hesitant to continue until I pressed her to do so.

"Go on girl," I urged her.

"Lady Julia is very lovely," she finished.

At once provoked and exasperated by her seeming cowardice I bit out a sharp reply. "That is a statement not a question and one which you have made on a previous occasion. Again Rose, if you are going to be brazen with me then you had better get on with it."

Pride ignited in those two dark pools of light that shone back at me from her eyes and I saw the gulf between maid and man breached before my own. It was only the smallest of movements, her head held just a little higher, her chin just a little firmer, but she would play the game. "When will you marry her?"

"Ha! I see you will take me at my word. I

told you before that that is none of your deuced business," I goaded and rebuked, but I had her now and knew she would persist.

"I am speaking out as you told me Sir," she replied, attempting contrition and innocence but achieving neither, her chin raised higher and her lip set firm.

"Well then Rose, you had best continue."

"She is your fiancée."

"My, my Rose, we are bold today." I could hear the mockery in my own words but could do nothing to prevent it."

"She won't go." She paused. "She won't go, despite…"

Like quicksilver she had lit the touchpaper and my temper flared red hot dissolving the entente that had existed between us only a moment before. My patience was quite gone, and I did not let her finish, there was only so much provocation I could take and clutching my stick with my good hand I stood abruptly and angrily faced away from her,

"Despite the fact that I am a cripple?" I rehearsed the words to the verandah window, then forced myself back to the girl to search her eyes for pity, allowing the rage to boil unchecked within me. But this time I had it well caged and would not let it out. Not this time. "You think she will have me in spite of my ruined body?"

Rose sprang from her perch, all insolence gone, she met my eye with a fire of her own, even took a step toward me though I could see keenly she did so against her fear. "No, Sir, no. That's not what I meant. Despite that you would send her away if you could. Despite that you would not love her." Her chin was raised and though her lip trembled she would be heard.

"What?" My anger was doused as quickly as it had flamed. This chit of a girl had unmanned me completely, taken my pity and thrown it back in my face – oh such bravery. I sat heavily back in my chair, barely keeping my laughter from bubbling free. How easily, passions raised, we had broken free of our classes. She would dare and I would allow it – no distinction between servant and master, maid and man. I was quite undone. "Oh Rose, Rose, you are a surprising creature. Sit back down and put your fear away. You know I will not harm you, no matter the provocation." And I would not.

"When did you stop pitying me? I asked abruptly. She shook her head in denial. "Rose, I know you girl, do not deny it. I swear to you that you have no need to pity my fiancée either. Though why I am attempting to explain this to you, heaven only knows," I finished.

"You love her then?" Her voice was no more

than a whisper.

"Yes Rose, I do. But marriage? Perhaps." With this last honesty the spell had broken, and I was the master once more, she the maid. "Now then girl you had better start practising before you say another word that will get you into more serious trouble." I shooed her towards the piano with my usual command, "And for God's sake play well!"

I let the music drift across me, taking me deep into my own thoughts as it always did, the melodies haunting and sweet and curative to my battered pride. I closed my eyes. Damn the girl.

I would fight it no longer. I would reaffirm my offer and ask Julia that very night to be my wife. I was determined. To gain her consent I would go down on my knees no matter the pain in my leg, no matter the indignity of having to ask my fiancée to help raise me back to my feet once my proposal was made. I stifled the laughter that that image provoked.

CHAPTER 40

A QUIET AFFAIR

Edward

The news of my intention to finally marry my fiancée was met with suffocating felicitations from my mother, gruff approval from my father and an altogether unexpected reaction from my brother Arthur.

"You should have sent her away," he announced coolly to me, well out of earshot of our parents.

I raised an eyebrow. "I tried brother; did you think I did not?"

"No," he replied firmly and paused, resolving momentarily to elucidate further. "That is disingenuous of me. Of course, you tried, but damn it man, what I mean to say is I like Julia, very much. Yes, very much indeed."

This was unexpected. I cocked my head in inquiry, for surely this was not something that had ever entered my head. He winced visibly at my reaction.

"No! No, Edward," he swiftly brushed aside my implied accusation. "I am not in love with your fiancée, but… Well, I just can't fathom what she can possibly get from the bargain." By this time his face had started to flush, the blush rising from his collar, already past his neck and threatening his cheek with an uncustomary puce-ness.

I smiled at my brother, strangely not in the least bit offended now that I had made my decision, but I was damned if I would let him know it, damned if I would ease his embarrassment just yet. "Do you think so little of me Arthur? Do you not think a woman capable of loving such a man as me?" I teased.

He flushed again, more violently. "God damn you, Edward. You are my brother and I love you dearly, you know perfectly well what I mean."

"Ah, you think that the fact that I am incapable of seeding a Mountfield heir to be a justifiable impediment to this marriage?"

"Well, I wouldn't exactly put it in those words," he choked out, momentarily appalled by my frankness.

I was exasperated by his graceless discomfiture. "You know that I cannot father a child with Julia or with any woman come to that but seeing as we are talking of that lady in particular, I swear to you for better or for worse

I am bound to her. Yes, perhaps it is selfish of me, but are we not all selfish creatures at heart? The girl is in love me and there is not a damned thing I can do to dissuade her. And just to make this crystal clear, I don't want to. I am weary of the fight, and if that makes me a selfish, inconsiderate blackguard in your eyes so be it. Cripple that I am, unworthy as you believe me to be, I do love her. It's that simple. As for producing an heir to preserve the family line, I'm afraid that is now entirely your responsibility, so you had best start looking for a wife and get on with it!" I couldn't keep the sneer from this last, no matter that I had tried.

Having rendered my brother temporarily speechless I held out my hand in truce. "Will you not shake my hand and congratulate me?"

Shamefaced he grasped my hand and shook it firmly. "Yes, well, I, I, most heartily wish you all the best, Edward. I hope you will be very happy together."

"Yes, yes," I dismissed him. "Seriously," I continued with more than a twinkle of amusement in my eye as I baited him, "Now that Mother has finally accomplished my impending nuptials, she will now transfer all her attentions to you. The family's honour depends upon it and I for one will seek out every opportunity to encourage her."

He clapped me on the back, drawing me into an awkward brotherly embrace. "Dear Lord, I hadn't thought of that," he murmured as we parted, a look of dismal realisation firmly stamped across his handsome red face.

Rapid preparations for the marriage occupied the household through the last days of Spring and the early days of Summer and by the beginning of June I had wed my fiancée Julia in a quiet ceremony attended only by mine and Julia's immediate family.

We went directly after the wedding breakfast to spend a month in the coastal resort of Southwold. Our days were occupied in long walks down by the sea's edge, where the wet sand favoured my injured leg in preference to the soft dry sands of the dunes that were to me largely impassable. Our nights brought with them a measure of intimacy that I had not thought possible, and I fervently prayed for the sake of my wife that it would prove enough.

The peace and comfort that we found in each other's company during those brief weeks was to set the tone of our married lives together. Away from Grange Park and the prying eyes of the servants, and most significantly my own mother and father, we were able to unwind, our friendship was allowed to strengthen and blossom and for the first time in many years I felt content. If I had been a religious man, my faith not battered by the war into a state of abeyant agnosticism, I would have seen my union with Julia as a strange kind of absolution, but whatever it was it was a release. I no longer viewed it as a selfish act, but simply for what it was, a marriage that she had entered into as willingly as I.

CHAPTER 41

HARVEST HOME

William

After the Mountfield wedding, June seemed to drag towards full Summer in a listless sonorous snore. The measured approach of the school summer holiday was dampened by sultry rain and throughout that long pregnant month, a month of anticipated freedom not yet realised, my sister was more and more absent from our lives. Lady Mountfield, no longer pre-occupied with her son's marriage preparations, had renewed her interest in her young protégé with an animated fervour. Rose practised longer and longer under her benefactress' tutelage as the days lengthened and mid-summer beckoned.

Finally, as June nudged against July and August beckoned the sense of release was palpable in every smiling young face. Every child tumbled out of the school room on that final day of term into the promised land of long, hot and sunny carefree days, when chores would be light, school a distant memory and freedom to roam was every village urchin's right.

Laughter was infectious where mischief was to be had, and I with only a brother to admonish my wilder antics, was pretty much left to my own devices that whole Summer through. I stayed out 'til late most nights and whilst my peers were often scolded for the lateness of their return to hearths by weary parents, I was most oftentimes berated with only the mildest of grunts and rebukes from Tom. The hours of work for my brother were long and grinding in the unaccustomed heat and he would come back fatigued and weary in no mood to reprove or reprimand.

There were evenings that I would unlatch the door, knowing full well that it was way past supper time and my brother, from his chair, would merely raise an eyebrow in my direction. "Have you caused mischief today lad that I need to know of?" he would ask, and I would shake my head vigorously in denial, though with a smile plastered across my face. He would harrumph a guttural response and then continue, "Well that's as I thought."

I would then fetch a plate of supper for myself and refill his own if it were empty and we would eat in companiable silence, sometimes with Rose, but most oftentimes not. Tom by this time had grown accustomed to Rose's unpunctuality but seemed reconciled to it at last. If she were very late, he would make comment, but not censure her.

The hot weather continued right through that Summer and the wheat baked in the fields under the sun's fiery gaze. The anticipated harvest would return an abundant yield and it would need all able hands to see the crop home. As one, all the men, women and children of the village would come together to see the task accomplished and I for one awaited that first day of labour with a growing sense of eagerness to begin.

I had not long to wait as that long dry Summer held its course over our little corner of England and the wheat continued to ripen, golden stalks swaying in rippling unison – a sea of flaxen softness dressing every field as far as the eye could reach. July dipped into August and as the early morning haze began to lift on the third Tuesday morning of that month, I stood a little apart as a small crowd began to gather in anticipation at the edge of Cooper's Field at the west end of the village. It was as if they had sensed the day was right, country folk all instinctually knowing by an empathy unspoken. They watched as old Mr Branton, the overseer who managed the Mountfield's farmlands, pressed for the hundredth time that Summer a few kernels between his thumb and forefinger finally releasing the white starch residue. He then turned to the assembled gathering of labourers and villagers and gave an abrupt nod confirming what they already knew. He looked up at the sun, "We'll start in an hour, when the dew's full burnt off." That was the cue for everyone to disperse, the women and children flying this way and that to spread the word, the men more at ease as they went to collect their tools.

Within the hour the horse-drawn binder, hired in for the harvesting, had been brought into the lane that on one side edged the first field. The machine was pulled by two coal-black dray horses with splashed white faces, forelocks and manes, their leather bridles and bits decorated with polished brass and standing more than a head above the tallest man, they were magnificent creatures. By this time, I had run to fetch my brother Tom and Daniel Martin and, as we watched Mr Branton and a line of farm labourers begin to open the field by hand, Tom turned to me with a cautionary smile. "You can help at the start lad but it's your task to bring our meals, mine and Dan's in place of Rose.

I wrinkled my nose in disgust and Tom reached down and laid his hand on my shoulder. "You know your sister can't be doing it, so it's fallen to you."

"Never mind Billy, your sister will be in time to fetch our last bite, for no doubt we'll be here 'til dusk each night." Dan winked at me. "You can stay by me and your brother then, can't he Tom and learn how it's done."

I looked up at my brother expectantly. "He knows full well how it's done, it's keeping him out of the way of getting pitched and stacked himself is what I'm worried about," teased my brother.

"He's but one small lad – I'm sure between the two of us we'll keep him out of mischief," Dan continued.

My brother put both hands on my shoulders and knelt down in front of me with a feigned degree of seriousness. "Alright Billy, but make sure you keep out of the way of the horses, they've got very big hooves!" The excitement of the day was surely infectious, my brother had most certainly caught it. In jest with me and his friend there was an unaccustomed lightness to his bearing that morning and I was determined to sustain it, recognising it for the rarity that it was in him. I answered with the biggest grin I could muster. He ruffled my hair, laughed loudly and then hoisted me up onto the gate so that I could get a better view of the cutting and stacking that had now begun in earnest. Each field would be started in the same way, a full length cut by hand before the cumbersome binder was pulled into the field and the mechanical process would start.

More men joined the first cutters with scythes and sickles, Dan Martin and my brother included, cutting and stacking the wheat into sheaves and bundling them together in larger stacks to cure in the sun. It was back-breaking work but there was a shared atmosphere of determination and camaraderie as the men toiled together in the morning sunlight. As soon as the first line was cut the binder made shorter work of the task and men concentrated solely on stacking and bundling. I watched from my gate post for nearly an hour until Tom pointed at the sun and motioned me away – my cue to go back to our house and fetch refreshments. I turned on my heel and raced back down the lane, returning much later with the other children and women who brought bread and cheese for the mid-morning break.

The hot meal of the day was carried to the fields at noon in cans and both my brother and his friend ate the stew that Rose had prepared the night before with relish. I sat with them in the stubble, eating my own portion and contentedly listening to the idle chatter. When it was time to return to their work, Tom pulled out a slip of paper from his pocket and carefully, with the stub end of a pencil, scribbled a note on it. "Take this to Rose, so she'll know where to come by and bring us our supper."

I took the note and Dan caught my hand as I went to go past him. "Come back at three, lad, for I'm sure the stacks from the first field'll be dry and ready to load by then. We'll ask if you can go on one of the carts and help out up there – less chance of you being pitch-forked that way."

True to his word, by the time I returned from my errands, Daniel Martin had somehow convinced Mr Branton into letting me ride on one of the stacking carts. It was exhausting work, but I was brim-full of pride to be working with the men, for I noted none of the other boys of my age from the village were allowed to help out. The sheaves were pitched onto the wagon from below and it was my task to stack them flat. Of course, I was only helping out the two experienced loaders and was unceremoniously thrown off the cart into the arms of my brother or Dan when they deemed the stack to have grown too tall for my safety. The best part was when the cart was fully loaded, and I was hauled back on top and although I was admonished to hold on for dear life, I was allowed to ride with the wagon to the stack yard.

By the time my sister arrived nearly three hours later my limbs ached, and my mouth was parched, and I was sure I was hungrier than I had ever been in my life. I spied her as I rode back from the stack yard and before the cart had even stopped, I was racing across the stubbled field to meet her.

"Well look at you Billy Baxter, doing a man's job now are you?" Her eyes sparkled as she started to set out the food and drink she had brought with her. "You've put me in a deal of trouble with Lady Mountfield, she was right put out that I had to come, but you'll never guess what happened…" she continued bursting with delight to tell her tale.

"Well girl, tell us, we're all ears." Dan Martin cut in.

"I would if you'd let me and not interrupt," she rounded on him.

As she spoke Tom grabbed her arm. "Peace, Rose and mind your manners," he admonished, "but by the look of you, you'd best spit it out before you choke on it, girl."

Not caring for his rebuke, Rose continued, "Lady Mountfield was just beginning to scold me for not coming to my practice, and you too Tom I might add, for 'tis you she blames for it, but then Sir Peter steps into the room and catches the start of what's to do and he starts bawling at her, and mind he sounded really angry. So she, that's Lady Mountfield, stops right there in mid speech like and Sir Peter turns to Lady Mountfield not caring that I'm there and he says to her…"

At this point Rose started to mimic the

master's voice and Tom and Dan and I could barely keep our laughter at bay. "...Damn it, woman, stop making a scene in front of the hired staff. The girl will go immediately and damn your bloody recital! The harvest will not wait, but you madam will."

"Then there was a great deal more shouting between the two of 'em, and I swear I didn't know where to look, and then Mr Mountfield, I mean Mr Edward that is, and Lady Julia and the butler and a whole lot of other servants who had heard the uproar came in to see if someone was being murdered like!"

"Then what happened?" urged Dan, clearly caught up in the story.

"Well not much else really as no-one was really being murdered, but it was Lady Julia sorted it out in the end."

"She's a brave one to step between 'em," commented Tom.

"She's really brave, I swear she is. She said that Sir Peter was right about the harvest, but Lady Mountfield was also right on account of her putting so much time and effort into her project being that it was all in the name of charity like. She said that that was a really fine thing and on account of that, the charity folk shouldn't suffer either. So, she says, that for the rest of the harvest she, Lady Julia that is, would bring your supper to you here."

"She said what?" Tom opened his mouth to say more then snapped it shut with incredulity. By this time Daniel Martin was howling with laughter.

"I swear I saw the master's eyes nearly pop out of his head when she said that, and that's when Mr Edward sorted everything out. He said that he would send one of the kitchen maids instead and that his wife would not need to trouble herself as he would arrange it himself. That's when Lady Mountfield got one of her headaches and Sir Peter seemed quite content as if nothing had ever happened, 'cepting he said Mr Edward was a sensible man and that..." Rose screwed up her face again and giving her best impression of Sir Peter continued, "clearly his sense comes solely from his father!" meaning himself, of course.

Tom just shook his head. "Well, I never did and all over a little bit of a thing like sup." He shook his head again. "After all that Rose, it best be a good supper you've brought is all I'll say," he said at last and this time everyone laughed. Even I could do nothing to check the silent tears of mirth as they slid down my face.

CHAPTER 42

THE BUTTERFLY

William

The harvest took nearly a week and a half to bring home and thankfully there had been no interruptions of rain, for the sun had beat steadily down that whole time ensuring that the crop was cut and stacked in the yard by the Friday of the second week. Pride and determination had accomplished the task in record time, and although all who had laboured on the land were bone weary there was contentment at a job well done. The purses of the working men were just a little heavier than usual on account of the long hours laboured – the dark night had been the only cause to halt the progress of the harvesting as dusk fell.

Saturday was to be a celebration for the whole village and preparations were well underway – fiddles tuned, dresses shaken out and shoes polished – and refreshments as in previous years were to be provided courtesy of the Grange Park kitchens. Rose would not be free to join the dance until well into the evening as that Saturday was co-incidentally chosen as the day of Lady Mountfield's charity recital. She had contrived to invite a small number of house guests who would stay with the family over the weekend and the party would also be swelled on the night by the Mountfield's more lowly associates such as the Reverend and Mrs Hawkins.

Rose was excited beyond belief and not least by the thought of wearing her new lace dress first to the recital and then later to the harvest dance. Lady Mountfield had surprised my sister with news of this gift only the day before and since then all her talk had been of how fine the garment was and how generous it had been of her benefactress to reward her with such a present. Tom had had his own views on the lavish gift, but wisely kept them to himself, but I had overheard him complaining to Dan how the 'gift' was more for the lady's benefit than my sister's. Esther Mountfield was a product of her class and on this night her protégé would look the part as well as play the part, for none of her assembled guests would countenance listening to a lowly maid, dressed in maid's garb. With the illusion of lace, my sister's own natural beauty and her uncommon skill, Lady Mountfield's beautiful butterfly would flutter her wings and tease and delight the sensibilities of that grand lady's acquaintance.

The recital was to start at 8pm in the drawing

room and Rose had begged both Tom and I to come and see her play, if only for the start, if only from outside. Lady Mountfield had indulged this desire of my sister and had benevolently proclaimed that if they were to stand outside the verandah for the first quarter of an hour, at a suitable distance of course, no-one in the family would consider it an impertinence. As a result, we found ourselves at 8 o'clock sharp, myself, Tom and Dan who had insisted on accompanying us, lingering at a discrete distance outside the open windows of the Mountfield's drawing room.

I crept a little closer so that I could better spy through the open windows, and I saw my sister enter the room to much excitement and much flustering from Lady Esther. Her pale cream dress hung to her sides in soft folds, the lace patterned with tiny, delicate flowers and around her neck she wore a string of pastel, pink-coloured beads, that were looped under a pretty collar of the same shade matching exactly the pinking of her lip. Her eyes shone with pure joy, as well they might, for I was sure I had never seen her look lovelier.

My brother came up behind me and rested a hand on my shoulder. "She looks a pretty picture don't she Billy?" he sighed and then reluctantly he continued, "Come a little further away now lad, they'll not be wanting you gawping at the window."

We returned to stand by my brother's friend who seemed to drink in my sister's every movement. "She looks a fine beauty in that get up Tom," he commented.

Tom punched him slightly with his balled-up fist right in the arm as if to jolt him out of his stare. "Dan, I swear, you're a fool for what a girl 'tis to look at. 'Tis nought but our Rose in a pretty frock, our Rose with her same silly notions, her same quick temper that you've been on the end of more than once, and her same sharp tongue. Stop staring like a fool and find some sense man."

"Right you are about her temper, right you are," Dan agreed with a wry shake of his head, but he carried on staring just the same.

Lady Mountfield had in the meantime introduced her protégé to her assembled guests, causing my sister to blush, curtsy quickly and seat herself at the piano. I knew by heart the music that she would play first – *Lacrimosa* – as she set her fingers to the keys, I closed my eyes imagining not the little gathering in the Mountfield's drawing room, but some far grander place. I imagined all kinds of fanciful scenes: music theatres, concert halls, opera houses, places where my sister's skill could soar aloft to the roaring approval of admiring onlookers. Such places, of course, were conjured all from my own fantasies, for truth be told I had no more idea what an opera house might look like than I could imagine the inside of a king's palace.

The music to my untrained ear was assuredly sweet and haunting, full of sorrow and melancholy, music that lingered, that called to the heart of the small boy that I was then. But it was not the tune itself that had affected me so, it was simply the thought that it was my sister who was playing it. My heart beat with pride and my smile stretched wide across my face.

"'Tis good I say, her playing," observed Dan Martin, "But 'tis not very cheery, sounds to me like dying."

"You're not wrong, but then 'tis not music for us, Dan. It's rich folks' music."

I saw the lie before my brother knew it himself. He was as enchanted with this music as I, but to save face with his friend against the notion of foolish sentiment he had spoken an untruth.

We listened for a short while more and then I let my brother steer me away from the verandah. We made our way across the moonlit lawn, rounded the pond and crossed the small orchard. We pressed on across fields, passing on our right a wild coppice of tall trees that marked the entrance to Grange Park wood, and finally approached the farm's outbuildings. Our destination was the large barn that served to store the hay after threshing. A few haystacks had been pulled out in front of the building, braziers had been lit, and round and about near the troughs extra buckets had been placed brim full of water against the need to douse any stray sparks that might let fly. Here and there men and women from the village sat about on the hay bales, watching their children run about whilst the fiddlers tuned their fiddles. At last couples stepped eagerly in front of the barn onto a cleared space that would serve as our dance floor. The music roared to life under nimble workman's fingers and the air was filled with the tunes of my childhood, brash, bold and heart-warming. The ale was passed around, the prepared feast savoured and praised, and the village celebration of harvest home was set to run long into the night.

My brother melted into the throng, and I slipped away, harbouring an uncharacteristic premonition that I should be at my sister's side, so I turned my back on the harvest cheer and stepped out once more towards Grange Park.

CHAPTER 43

A GRAND SOIRÉE

Edward

My mother's creature was ushered into the drawing room with much pomp and ceremony, my mother drinking in the light applause that accompanied her brief introduction. The girl herself looked awkward in the limelight, though her eyes shone despite her nerves. My mother had her decked out in a cream lace dress, though simply cut I'm sure the garment was by far the most expensive piece of cloth that had ever touched Rose's pale flesh. Around her neck, my mother had decked her out with a single string of beads, pink as the child's lips and matching the slight flush on her cheek. I must confess she looked a bewitching angel, dressed in lace and innocence, my mother's butterfly flexed her gentle wings although she had not yet set a finger to the keys.

Biding to one corner of the room and seated in one of the drawing room's more comfortable chairs my father, having already dosed himself liberally with wine during the meal, was proving to be a more jovial host than I had anticipated. He was uncharacteristically polite to my mother in front of the assembled gathering, condescendingly complimenting her for, in his words, 'the raising up of her latest protégé'. For him the recital could not be completed soon enough, but he was equally happy to accept the plaudits for his encouragement of his wife in this enterprise.

"Yes, father has been very supportive of Mother," commented my brother Arthur, throwing a knowing smirk towards Julia and myself at telling this preposterous lie.

As Rose began to play, the assembled guests at first continued their conversations until slowly, assuredly all fell silent – such was the quality of the music, the lightness of her touch, the passion of her playing. Wrapped up in the music as I was, the time seemed to pass so very quickly and before I had time to take a breath, she had played her last piece. Of all the pieces played that night it was the first, the *Lacrimosa* that had captured me most fully. It was achingly beautiful music that seemed to arrest the heart and in some small measure I was resentful for having had to share it with my mother's boorish friends, much preferring the lazy afternoons of practice where I could imagine the girl played solely for me.

The Reverend and Mrs Hawkins, having known Rose all her life, were the most complimentary of her talent, but even they awarded my mother the lion's share of their praise for her outstanding accomplishment in raising this poor child upward. My mother and father's friends, undoubtedly moved by the performance, chose to follow the usual class mores and applaud the benefactress' rather than acknowledge the vessel of her benevolence too keenly.

"You play very prettily my dear," remarked Lady Fanshaw to Rose at the end of the recital, "I am sure you are very grateful to Lady Mountfield for her kindness."

"Yes, Ma'am, I truly am," replied Rose.

"Good girl," continued Lady Fanshaw and then turned abruptly to her companions without another word.

It was of course left for Julia to ease any discomfort in Rose, in awe as she was of the grand ladies and gentlemen. "Lady Mountfield, I think it is time for Rose to be excused for the night. You may recall there is the village dance tonight and I am sure she is eager to join in the merriment."

"Dear me yes, bless you Julia for thinking of it. Do run along now Rose, you have made me very proud tonight, very proud. You have truly repaid my many kindnesses to you with your recital. Now run along dear, before you get in anyone's way." And so it was that after having displayed such exquisite skill, charmed her noble audience, and made her benefactress proud, the girl was dismissed, like the servant she was, out into night.

CHAPTER 44

CROSSING THE RUBICON

William

Returning in time to hear the last dulcet tones of Rose's recital, I watched from the little hedge by the pond as my sister stood up from her stool. She was quickly surrounded by the fine ladies and gentlemen of Lady Mountfield's acquaintance but cut a small figure despite her pretty clothes that made her only outwardly one with them. Soon the chatter of the fine company returned each unto the other and my sister stood somewhat apart, a little bewildered as to what she should do next. I said a silent prayer of thanks as Lady Julia, kind and thoughtful as ever, took my sister by the hand, rescuing her from her unusual predicament.

I had expected Rose to emerge from the verandah windows and waited some several long minutes before realising that she must have left by way of the door to the hall. From there she would pass through the servant's quarters, next through the kitchen and then appear from the rear of the property which I surmised would take several minutes more. I waited patiently expecting her to appear at any moment from around the side of the house. At length I decided to move closer to the drawing room to reassure myself that she had indeed departed. I crept quietly along the side of the hedge by the lawn until I had a better view, but she was nowhere to be seen. She must have been swifter than I had anticipated and already be well on her way.

Quickly and stealthily, I retraced my steps, dipping low as I ran along the moonlit lawn back towards the pond. From there I pressed on toward the orchard, emerging from the little stand of fruit trees in time to see my sister already running across the first of the fields. Fleet of foot and light as air, she tripped along, dancing and spinning under the moonlight, joyful for the night and the music but surely eager to join the party with her own folk. Slowing my pace, I took my time to smile at my beautiful sister.

As she approached the dark coppice, there waiting for her was my brother's friend. He leaned against one of the trees, the darkness casting him half in shadow. She stopped abruptly, clearly disquieted by his appearance and, as I moved closer, I watched as he offered her his arm. Clearly she was not in the mood to accept his escort, and shook her head, even in the dwindling light I could see her anger flared. Next, he grasped her hand and she tried unsuccessfully to shrug him off. My heart pounded in earnest as I saw him pull her, against her nay-saying, into the heart of the dark wood. Did I dare to follow?

Knowing I was no match for Daniel Martin and fearing his intent I determined to fetch my brother. The barn was only a little way off by this time and I pounded my legs hard as I skirted the wood and ran straight into the village gathering. I spotted my brother almost at once, but he was in the midst of a lively dance, and I could not attract his attention. I must have taken a misstep as I stumbled and blundered into Mr Barton.

"Steady on there, lad, what's set you in such a hurry?" he said picking me up and dusting me down. My growing sense of fear and panic must have showed on my face for he compelled me more forcefully to make myself clear. "What's wrong Billy lad? Show me boy."

My chest was heaving by this point and as I pointed back towards the wood, I fought to force words from my silent lips. "R – R – Rose." I breathed out at last. "T- Tom. F – Fetch Tom." I continued to press the words from my mouth. Pointing once again towards the wood and trusting that Mr Barton would fetch my brother, I sprinted back the way I had come.

Time dragged slowly at odds with my frantic

pace, as I raced through the trees searching for my sister and Daniel.

I found them at last hidden deep in the thickest part of the wood, for he must have dragged her quite a distance. There was barely any light to see by, but I heard her frightened fearful voice pleading with the man to let her go.

"Nay, don't, Daniel. For pity's sake leave me be. I want… I want to get to the dance. Let me go. I don't like it here, I say."

"Don't say so Rose. 'Tis only you I want. Kiss me pretty, Rose. Just one kiss. What a pretty girl you are in your fine fancy dress. Kiss me pretty, Rose," he almost begged, but there was anger too in his voice.

Nearly upon them I watched with a child's alarm as Daniel Martin pressed his lips against her mouth. I watched as she tried to push him away with all her might as he messed with her hair, pulled at her dress, held the delicate lace of it in his too big, too gruff hands.

"St – Stop it!" I whispered. "Stop it!" I said again, this time louder.

Startled from his intent and my re-discovered voice, Daniel Martin, whilst keeping a hand on my sister's arm, grabbed me up by the collar and pulled me towards his face. "Go home, Billy! We're talking is all. Just me and your sister."

"S – She, d – doesn't, want you!" I choked, all the while trying to prize his hand away from my collar. I must have cuffed him in my struggle, for his face transformed into one of pure rage. I heard my sister's screams as he raised his fist to my face and felt the full force of the blow to my head.

When I awoke there was no sign of Daniel Martin, no sign of my sister. I do not know how long I must have lain there unconscious but as I pulled myself to my feet, I heard the distant sound of laughing voices. I picked my way towards that sound, half-stumbling and swaying, feeling now the full force of Daniel Martin's blow, my face throbbing painfully and tasting the tang of blood on my tongue.

"Are you sure this is a good idea, Arthur?" I heard Mr Edward ask as I forced myself on further.

"Don't tell me you were enjoying Mother's preening and all that sanctimonious claptrap that her cronies were spouting. I'm sure we will have a much grander time with the common folk, don't you Julia? I think it was a splendid idea of mine to steal away to the har…"

He stopped mid-sentence as I staggered at last from the bushes. "Rose!" I half-begged, half-cried, "Rose…" Instantly Julia Asgarth was at my side, clearing the hair from my eyes, wiping the tears from my face that I did not know were falling.

The young master knelt down on his un-injured leg and with my broken speech I made him understand what had transpired. As I was hastily finishing my tale, my brother Tom, accompanied by Mr Barton, and several more of the villagers came upon us.

With a haste born of dreadful urgency two search parties were quickly assembled, my brother would lead one and Arthur Mountfield the second. Torches were hurriedly brought by, and the two parties set out to find my sister. I did not want to leave, but Lady Julia and the young master persuaded me to go with them, accompanied by several of the village women, to wait back at the big house.

CHAPTER 45

VIGIL

Edward

Lady Mountfield's soirée was interrupted by the sombre sight of our little party trudging back across the lawn and entering en masse through the verandah window.

"What is the meaning of this Edward?" demanded my mother, my father's ire threatening to follow in an explosive outburst of his own.

"Peace, Mother, now is not the time," I cut them both off sharply, "There has been a terrible incident. Right this moment Arthur is out searching with the lad's brother for this poor child's sister," I replied indicating the boy, Billy who was sat half in, half out of the verandah door, my wife Julia sitting stoically by his side.

"For Rose?" my mother queried anxiously.

"Yes, for Rose." I replied. After a brief explanation of what had occurred the mood in the room turned grave. My mother's guests grouped themselves together talking in hushed tones, whilst the villagers gathered themselves just outside on the patio. My father and mother, for once united in their task, both took to ordering the servants, ensuring that tea and other refreshments were organised for those who were already here and for those who were to come. My father took it upon himself to phoneced the local police station and was assured that officers would be dispatched forthwith.

Sitting next to my wife, his legs drawn up to his chest and his arms wrapped tightly around his knees, the young lad kept his silent, shocked vigil, eyes fixed on the dark gardens, alert to any signs of light emerging from the gloom.

It was a little after midnight when the first weary party of searchers returned to Grange Park. Tom Baxter had been urged to give up the hunt only once the torches had started to burn low, but he was determined to go back out as soon as more could be fetched. The little party reported that their search had as yet proved fruitless, with not one trace of Rose or Daniel Martin being found. Cups of warm tea were pressed on them and once dispensed with the party started to ready themselves to resume their search.

"Look!" shouted one of the villagers who was furthest away from the open verandah doors.

"I see torches, and I think they be carrying someone. Praise God let it be so!"

Despairingly, heart-breakingly there was to be no good end to this affair. As the second party approached, I saw my brother Arthur walking stiffly with the lifeless form of Rose carried in his arms. Though her dress was torn, her arms scratched and blooded, she looked for all the world as if she were merely sleeping.

Grasping my cane in my hand, I hurried awkwardly to reach Arthur as quickly as I could, Tom Baxter and his brother strangely trailing me as if they did not want to know the outcome, and indeed who would want to know this truth?

"Is she?" I let the words hang in the air.

My brother gave a curt nod of his head, and it was then that I saw the discoloured bruising around the poor girl's throat.

Behind me I heard Tom howl out his despair, sinking to the ground on his knees and the soft, gentle whimpers of the little boy who had tried and failed to defend his sister. I felt bile rise in my gut, transfixed as I was on the thought of such brutal and senseless cruelty enacted upon so pure and fierce a soul.

CHAPTER 46

FRACTURE

William

Experience has taught me that time does not bring true solace only distance. Thinking back on that terrible night it is for Tom that my heart truly bleeds. I watched as my proud, strong brother sank to the ground, to his knees, his head miserably dropped in his hands. He could not trust the flow of his tears, tears for Rose, tears for himself, for the life he had known 'til this day and further much further. Surely his thoughts had drifted wider than our own small grief for such was the visceral roar of sorrow that he howled into the night. Did he in those brief moments remember all the men he had seen lost, friend and foe that the Great War had ripped away? Did he cry out at the betrayal of his friend, for the senseless loss of our father and the swift cruel death of our mother Lily, and finally did he rail out once more his grief as he returned to the unalterable sight of our dear Rose, her poor shattered body raw before his eyes? Gulping sobs came from his lips as he wept out her name over and over.

It was not what any of the fine men and ladies could bear to watch, save for Edward and Arthur who had breathed atrocity first-hand in the Great War, but we all knew. I was drawn towards this miserable sight, I pushed my way forward, tears flowing as freely as those of my brother, and I crouched down beside him. I reached my small arms around him trying to comfort him. And then more arms followed, strong men that I had known all my life, trying to get through to Tom, there were many words to soothe, no condemnation, no pity, just the kindness of friends who understood. I let these men take my brother, slowly bringing him back from the howling beast he had become, slowly bringing him back to the man he was.

Sluggishly, now a little apart from the men, I got back to my feet, lifted my head, then lifted my eyes to search until I found the face I was looking for.

She stepped away from the fine men and ladies, she stepped away from Edward's side and came towards me. Systematically she put her arms around my dirty clothes, my ragged body and hugged me as strongly as her delicate frame would allow. I clung to her fiercely, the scent of lavender filling my senses, my tears staining her fine cotton dress, but she had no care of that. She was to me in that instant the mother I had lost, the mother that I needed to try and rock away my sorrow and ease my grief. Her eyes, if I had seen them, would surely have sparkled with fierce determination reflecting back to me a growing love for this poor man's son.

I did not know it then, but my future shifted in that moment with Julia Asgarth's realisation that I would become the child she could not have, would never have from her own body, the child that needed her as a drowning man needs air to breathe. This one act changed everything.

I reached for her, my tears in her lap, whispering my sister's name, my mother's name, her name. Whispering, whispering, the words flowing freely at last, hearing at last the soft, small sound of my own voice; Rose, Lily, Julia, Rose, Lily, Julia, Rose…

Remembering nothing from that moment on, it was only much later I learned how Doctor Horton had patiently explained my reaction to Julia and Edward. He reassured them that shock had finally overtaken me and brought on sleep. I needed no draught to soothe me, sleep was for me the anaesthetic to the monstrous sight I had witnessed and the aching pain I felt.

CHAPTER 47

AFTERMATH

Edward

Rose Baxter was buried in the churchyard of Long Wendon, next the church in which she had been christened. It was a simple service after which all repaired to the village hall for the funeral feast, for there was not enough room at Tom's small home for all who wished to attend. The cold victuals were sent as a courtesy by my mother and father; and myself, Julia and Arthur attended both the funeral and the feast, though my parents only attended the former.

The service and funeral feast were rituals to be endured only lightened by the unlikely intervention of Mr Scrivens who had insisted on having the piano wheeled to the hall and tuned in preparation. Partway through the proceedings the piano master turned schoolteacher got up and began to play some of the fine music compositions that Rose herself had been tutored to play, a poignant reminder of her uncommon gift.

Though the police had set out to find Daniel Martin, nothing had been heard of him for several weeks. In the end everyone agreed that it was a mercy when he finally turned up drowned. It was never discovered quite how he had come to his untimely end, whether an accident or by his own hand, but it certainly spared the family the further heartache of a trial, and ultimately spared Daniel Martin the notoriety of the hangman's noose.

Days turned into weeks and things began to return to normal: the holidays were now ended, and the children trooped back to school and Billy, though there was less reason for his presence now his sister was gone, was seen more and more about the estate. He shadowed my wife, encouraged by her good self and their quiet, unusual friendship seemed of benefit to both their spirits. The previously straightened relationship between my parents had somewhat eased, the events of late having brought them to a better accord, something akin to their younger selves. My mother's headaches had all but disappeared and my father's criticisms were no-longer so mean-spirited.

Mother had had the piano moved out of the drawing room, assuming that it was too prominent a reminder for all concerned, but this action was very quickly reversed.

One day in late October, Julia and Billy

were walking across the lawn in animated conversation, whilst I was sitting in a lazy chair in the drawing room taking in the last of the afternoon sun. They were approaching the open windows when the boy stopped abruptly, clearly upset by what he saw.

"Where is it?" he asked, "It should be here, 'tis not right without it here," he stammered.

"What's the boy saying, Edward?" chipped in my father who was sat further into the room completing his crossword.

"I think he means the piano," replied Julia, solicitous of Billy's rising distress.

That was all the catalyst needed for another upheaval. On ascertaining that the boy wanted to see the piano in its rightful place, my father inexplicably set the reversal in motion. Staff were called and the piano was very quickly restored to the drawing room. He even went so far as to encourage the boy to play trying very hard not to wince when Billy, by no means possessing the skill of his sister, began to thump out a tune on the keys.

Instead of raging at the child he simply ruffled his hair, though tentatively as if he did not know how clean the boy's head to be, then promptly moved to sit in a chair further away and resumed his abandoned crossword. "There's a good, lad," he said as he retreated. "Esther dear," he continued, "Show him how to play a little quieter would you?"

Both myself and Julia were in awe of this little drama playing out, hardly able to contain our laughter at my parent's extraordinary indulgence of the village boy. My mother had by this time approached Billy and, trying very hard to make herself sound less imperious, was showing him how to lay his hands more gently on the notes to tease out the music.

Just as they had allowed Rose into the drawing room to practice, my mother and father now did the same for Billy. Over the ensuing weeks his clumsy renditions of *All Things Bright and Beautiful*, interspersed with popular hits like *When Father Papered the Parlour*, garnered wincing smiles from my parents and suppressed chuckles from myself and Julia at their discomfiture. His playing was crude and rudimentary at best, but somehow it proved a balm to us all, the servants often lingering longer in their duties to watch the boy with wistful smiles of their own.

Tom Baxter was the only one amongst us who could not seem to rally himself out of his gloom and would often cut a brooding presence as he went about his duties. Even Billy could not seem to raise his spirits and I surmised that their evenings at home in the cottage must have been joyless and drear at best.

CHAPTER 48

ARRANGEMENTS

Edward

I was instantly aware of Tom Baxter's awkwardness as he stood in the centre of the drawing room at Grange Park, the opulence of the surroundings unnerved him. This place offered him no comfort, the closed lid of the piano a sombre reminder of why we were all here. With hindsight perhaps my mother should have attended the funeral feast in the village hall, but instead she had wanted to mark Rose's parting in her own way, at a distance from the tragic event itself and with close acquaintances at a private memorial. I thought it curious that she would invite Tom Baxter, but perhaps she supposed that the presence of the Reverend Hawkins, who was of our party, might offer him comfort, for even she had recognised how changed the man was, unable to lift himself from the pervading darkness of his thoughts.

Billy, a little perplexed at the reason for this gathering, for it was a full two months since his sister's passing, stood close by my wife and she in turn took pains to occupy him.

My father had acceded without complaint to the request for this gathering and was now engaged in quiet conversation with the Reverend. It was in no small measure remarkable that the shocking events that had occurred had mellowed his recollection of the girl to fondness, a girl whose presence at Grange Park he had so often disparaged and despised. He had acted with decorum, greeting everyone with a landowner's sense of propriety and I for one was glad of it.

I approached the older brother with my arm extended to encompass his shoulder and steer him towards the door. On reflection this could have seemed comical to anyone choosing at that moment to look towards us – the cripple with the cane offering support to the able-bodied man. "Tom, let us find somewhere quieter to talk, for there is something I would discuss with you." With a curt nod of acknowledgement, he allowed me to steer him from the room and into the study father along the hall.

"Please sit down." I gestured to the armchair nearest to where the hearth fire was lit despite the unseasonable mildness of this late October day. I poured two stiff drinks and handed one to Tom as he sat, returning to the cabinet to retrieve my own, for I could not juggle two glasses with my one free hand. I sat in the opposite chair and in silence we drank our brandy.

At length Tom's attention rallied. "What did you want to talk about, Sir?"

"I need to know of your plans for the future," I replied, not quite sure how to proceed now the moment had arrived.

"Plans? I don't rightly know what you mean Sir, 'cepting my plans are what they always were, to work with Mr Frances as I have since I've come back."

I noted the word he said was back not home and I pitied him for it. A flicker of doubt passed across his face then. "Sir, do you mean there's no place for me here, does Mr Frances not make good report of me?"

"No, Tom, no," I reassured him swiftly. "Do not imagine insult where there is none intended. Your diligence to your employ is not in the slightest doubt. Mr Frances says you are an able and most capable worker and I believe him to be a true and honest fellow in his account. Believe me when I tell you that is not what I meant at all."

"Sir, then what?" he asked flatly.

"I merely sought to enquire whether your heart is in it, for I had heard," I continued cautiously, "That it was your earnest wish to go abroad to the Americas or perhaps Australia. Both Billy and Rose had spoken of it you see…"

He flinched slightly at mention of his sister's name, it was no more than a soft intake of breath, an involuntary movement that spoke volumes to the man's state of mind. His eyes showed his astonishment at this confession of his sister, "Rose, she said... she told you; she told you this?"

"It was something that she spoke of quite often. I think she would have wanted you to go. With all that has passed, is it not time that you thought a little of yourself?"

"I can't Sir, 't'wouldn't be right on the boy." There was both exasperation and bluntness in his reply. His sense of duty had reaffirmed itself, the same duty that had seen him remain here these many months, doing a job he doubtless cared little for, his sense of responsibility keeping him in Long Wendon when his heart looked firmly towards other places and other lands. Could he be persuaded otherwise? I did not know.

"If there were a way, would you consider it? I pressed.

In the silence that ensued I stood and went to retrieve the decanter of brandy, and with a shaking hand splashed more of the bronze-coloured spirit into both our glasses. I set it on the table beside me, sat back down and allowed the smooth taste of the alcohol to wash over my palate like anaesthetic, the pain in my leg dulled a little more.

I watched him take a mouthful from his own glass and measured my question to him. "Tell me honestly, is that where your heart is set? Speak up man."

"If things were different, which they ain't, my answer is yes, I would go. I'd been set to go when I turned eighteen and had my dad's blessing."

"And then the war came," I finished his thought, "And you felt an obligation to raise your sister and brother in your father's stead."

"Who else?" he asked startled. "I don't regret it, Sir, don't think that of me. They're my own kin and I'd never leave them be, not like our Susan did."

"Your honour is not in question, Tom," I brushed his duty aside with my hand, "But Rose is gone and staying here the rest of your days won't bring her back."

He lifted his sad tormented eyes towards me and in that moment my compassion was all for this broken man who sat before me.

"You must go Tom. You must." I said simply.

"'Tis impossible, Sir, Billy…" He took another mouthful of the brandy, sucked it in with air through his teeth.

"How do you know that Billy wouldn't want to

go with you?" Clearly, he had not thought of this. I pressed on, "And if he did not, he would always have a place here, at Grange Park, a home even."

"Sir?" He looked up, uncomprehending.

"My wife is very fond of the boy," I began.

"She is a kind lady Sir, and I'm thankful, but..."

He paused and I pressed on. "She is more than fond Tom."

"Yes, Sir. I can see that she is. Sometimes I see them thick as thieves like and wonder what he's got to talk about now he's found his voice. He tries to talk to me too sometimes, but I don't know how it happens – it's almost as if I spoils it, I just look on him Sir and I see her, I see her and I can't, I just clam up like." The drink had loosened his talk and I could see plainly on his face the guilt he kept locked up inside him.

"You couldn't know what Daniel Martin would do, Tom, no-one could." I tried to reassure him.

"I should have known damn it! Begging your pardon, Sir..."

I waved him off. "There's nothing to forgive."

"He told me he'd taken a liking to her; I should have known it was more than that. I should have seen the way he looked at her..."

"Stop right there, man," I said rising from my seat and clasping him by the elbow, forcing him to look me in the face. "How could you have known what was in that man's heart? How could anyone have known?"

Sinking further back into his chair he took another mouthful of the brandy I had forced on him. I splashed more into his glass and my own and retook my seat.

"Happen you're right, but he was my friend, I trusted him…"

"And he failed you." I finished for him. "The guilt is no-one's but his own."

We sat in silence a while longer, each of us contemplating the truth of it, each wondering if somehow things could have turned out differently. At length he seemed to relax a little more, sighing he scratched his head.

"She really do like the boy, don't she, your lady. Right fond of him, who can fathom that?" he mused.

"As I said, she is more than fond Tom."

"Yes Sir, I reckon you're right. More than fond." I waited for the idea to work its own way through to him.

"We can never have children of our own." The words had passed my lips on a single breath, and I saw his confusion disappear, to be replaced by what? Guilt again, or guilt mixed with gratitude, did he sense his own weakness, did he recognise the possibility of a weight lifting from him? Surely all those powerful feelings and more twisted and raged inside him.

We talked long into the evening; we talked as the evening advanced quickly into night and all the while Tom Baxter brooded his future. As we chased the remaining shadows of the night towards the dawn, Tom's mind seemed to sway in one direction and then the next as he weighed up what I was asking. Could this brother give up his kin and let the man who sat before him raise him as his own? Could he reconcile his choice, assuage the guilt that assuredly nipped at his sense of duty, overcome it and choose myself and my wife to give his brother a different, perhaps a better life?

As the hour drew dark, the brandy had emboldened his spirit. "They watched her, Sir."

"Tom?"

"Always they watched her. From when she was little, like. She were different, like as she was some fairy child. Sometimes the way she held herself like she was too proud for us, like she could do anything Sir and then she grew, and well, I knew she were lovely, and I thought... I thought what had passed, the war, my dad, that it wouldn't matter... that she would be, I don't know, that she would be alright. I couldn't make her out sometimes, Sir." The words had tumbled from his mouth unbidden.

"Is that why you were so hard on her?"

"Yes, No! She were a pretty girl and a poor one Sir. My mother said that were a mix of trouble waiting. But I thought, I thought she were so strong and that she would be alright. I thought that them that watched her, them that looked at her, was all on account of her pretty face but now I think on't they wanted her. Yes, that's it, they wanted her."

"Tom, stop. That's not true at all. Do not make the mistake of judging all others by the actions of one man. These fancies are brought on by grief, nothing more." But were they? I checked myself. I moved towards him, put a hand on his arm to offer comfort and he raised his eyes to mine.

"Did you want her?" he spoke those words on the smallest of breaths.

I backed away. "No, God, no, I swear to you," I exclaimed perhaps too forcefully.

He retracted the question as quickly as it had flown from his lips. "I meant no harm, Sir, I just…"

"You need to be sure." I waved his apology aside and struggled for fairness to guide my answer, to not let my affront and revulsion to grow anger inside me. If not for my ruined body, could I, would I have wanted this girl? Did I not, after all, possess the same feelings and desires as any able-bodied man? I questioned myself rigorously, searching where I did not want to look. Had there at any point in my relationship with Rose been an unnatural hunger or intent? I replied stiffly, firmly. "These things should always be clear. I am no Daniel Martin. I did not want your sister, not like that, never like that."

I turned away from him. My conscience was clear, I told myself it was the truth, but was I certain? Once again, I forced the idea into my mind, past the revulsion. And there it was, the truth, I had watched her, I had watched her like a butterfly, a pretty, precious butterfly. Just like my mother had collected this beautiful girl and nurtured her extraordinary talent, just like Daniel Martin who had looked and wanted and taken where his obsession had led him. But had my intention been the same as Daniel Martin's? No, it could never be, the very idea was monstrous. Tom Baxter, drunk with his own pain and the fine brandy I had plied him with had forced this surety on me and I thank God he did. I had examined my heart and knew for certain I was no monster.

Tom raked his hand through his hair, shrinking back inside himself, heedful now of his position; the humble servant, the poor man's son and all I could feel was pity for him. I would ease his pain if I could. I sat once again in my chair and forced him to hold my gaze.

"She was a child, a beautiful child who possessed an uncommon skill. I admired her talent; I admired her spirit and I wish to God she was not gone." Wishing to explain myself further I took a breath and continued, "But that's not all, she meant much more to me than that. Your sister looked past my ruined face and body and instead of offering me pity she gave me fire. After I had heard her play, most oftentimes I would ask her to stay and talk with me. Just talk, nothing more. She had an unhealthy disregard for her elders and betters did Rose."

At this Tom Baxter snorted, "You're not wrong there, Sir."

"When we talked, I commanded her to always speak the truth. At first, I confess, she was a curiosity to me, but later on I found I liked the way she challenged me. Simply put man, and this is not something a man likes to admit even to himself, your small slip of a sister gave me back a measure of courage."

"How so, Sir?" Tom Baxter was now hooked on my brandy-fuelled confession.

"As I said she was one of a very few who did not pity my condition and she would not let me pity myself. She all but delivered me my wife, all wrapped up in a bow."

By this time Tom was all agog. "How?" he

choked out.

"She simply told me I was fool to keep refusing Julia, not in so many words, but she was damned right, I was being a fool. Oh, she was very bold your sister."

By the time I had finished we were both roaring with laughter, not master and servant, just two proud men with matching tears running down our faces. I reflected on my own sense of loss in that moment. Her music had spoken first to my heart, but it was her fearless nature that had given back to this poor war-ruined creature a part of his soul.

With an unsteady gait Tom got to his feet. Swaying a little too much he held out his hand and absurdly I took it. "Billy should stay."

"When will you leave?"

"A week or two, I reckon. Will you do something for me?"

"Of course."

"Tell him after I've gone."

It was all settled in the following weeks. There were no fond farewells, one day Tom Baxter was here and the next he was gone. Or course I paid for his passage and pressed a few notes on him, but he would not take much, he was a proud man, an honourable man. I accompanied him to the station and reassured him most forcefully that he was doing the best for the boy. I did not want him to carry any misplaced feelings of guilt on that long voyage and I remain hopeful to this day that he did not.

Julia and I formerly adopted Billy (William) Baxter and he became our own child to love and to care for. And as for my father? As you can imagine he received the news of our new family arrangement with a grudging acceptance and promptly instructed his solicitor to change his will, naming my brother Arthur as sole inheritor of his estate on his death but with a codicil that my wife and I should remain at Grange Park for as long as our lives allowed. Thus, for the first time in my life, save for my army stipend, I earned a wage as the estate manager of my family's ancestral home.

1939

THE PRESENT

CHAPTER 49

A FAMILY PORTRAIT

William

Time has run short, my commission arrived a little over two months past and I am now in receipt of my posting, having passed without incident through my basic training.

I have chosen to come alone to Grange Park, to return to the stone walls that are now as familiar to me as breathing, a place of sorrow and joy in equal measure, but of late a place that has known more of the latter. There are things that have been left unsaid between us, my mother and father and I, for that is now who they have become, grown into my heart through Julia's quiet gentleness and Edward's pale reflection of her love, though perhaps he would not even admit this to himself.

There are questions still to be answered, I need to understand why my brother left England after my sister's death, and why there has been no contact with Tom down all these long years since.

Edward Mountfield is a little astonished at my questions, surprised that I have kept silent. Surprised, perhaps, that I even have these concerns at all.

"There is no great mystery, William," he announces. "You were ten years old. Tom was nearly broken, he needed to leave and quickly, that much was clear to everyone. Your brother knew that with Julia you would be in safer hands than if you journeyed with him."

He pauses. I look for more and he continues: "Your sister had confided on many occasions of Tom's desire to go abroad before the war, before all this craziness and then there was Julia herself."

"I can understand it from my brother's point of view – that he thought he was acting in my best interests, but…." I reply.

"He did not leave you lightly."

"No of course, that is not what I meant."

"William, do you think we took you in for charity's sake? Is that why you have not asked this of me before?" There is a flash of anger and impatience in his voice.

I can see the confusion, the astonishment, perhaps even the hurt in his eyes.

"No, at first, I don't know."

He grips his stick more firmly and gestures for me to help him to his chair. I ease him down and then pull up a chair myself and sit facing him.

"Julia needed you as much as you needed her. I thought you understood." I am not sure that I agree with him, but I let it pass.

"And you?" The question hangs between us.

"For Rose," it is almost a whisper, "I made you my son for Rose." He puts his head in his hands and I fear that he will cry, but he does not, men of his world do not show their emotions so easily. And then he smiles and I see his eyes are glazed with a memory. Momentarily he returns to me, his smile still firmly in place and he shakes his head.

"Do you know, I don't even think I told your mother this, though now I recall the conversation I did make confession to your brother." He seems surprised by his own admission. "Your sister near as damn it told me to marry Julia." Seeing my reaction he continues. "Oh, she was bold your sister. You have much of her spirit, William, though in you it reveals itself differently perhaps in your quiet determination to succeed." He has said his peace and curiously for me it is enough. My questions of a moment ago, those that I have carried with me down the years, no longer seem important.

My mother, Julia comes out onto the patio at

that moment with a tray of tea things. She is not one for fuss and would always prefer to sort for herself than to call on others for assistance.

"Really Julia, the staff must wonder sometimes what we pay them for."

"Nonsense my dear, they are busy enough."

I take the tea tray from her, set it down on the table and begin to pour for the three of us.

"Just as you say my dear."

I sit back down in my chair and sip the strong tea, content to enjoy this brief hour spent in their company, as if the world has all but stopped.

I take note, as always, of the care they show one another, witnessing the resolution of the conflict that had once raged between them: Edward Mountfield's resolve to lead a martyred single life and Julia's resolve to spare him that fate. She has won that private battle, as I see them now, he resting his injured leg, while she puts a blanket over his legs and tucks it fondly in. I see the soft touch of their hands, all affection between them on show, there is no distinction in public and in private, for it is all the intimacy they have known in their near twenty years of marriage, and it is all that is needed.

"It's getting late Edward." My mother starts to clear the tea things away.

"I'd best get back." As I rise, I continue, "You

will come tomorrow?"

"Oh William, of course we will come," my mother admonishes.

My father stands and I see the pain still bites as it has done for him down all the long years. I see the expression on my mother's face, her heart still bleeds as she puts down the tray and offers him her arm.

"Perhaps you are right dear. I should leave the cups and saucers for Jessica to clear away."

With the last warmth of the sun's heat on my back I make my way across the fields, then down the well-worn track to the village. I will see them again before I depart.

CHAPTER 50

TRAIN TO WAR

William

We go to the train station. Goodbyes from all. My mother kisses me like any mother would – she could not have been better; my son and daughter are the grandchildren she would have never had but for my sister Rose. I know I will return. And the romance of that knowledge gives me hope.

I turn to my father, and he shakes me firmly by the hand. His other hand rests as ever on the cane that helps him to stand. He keeps my hand gripped a little longer in his. He is a man of few words, and this suits us both and, in that moment, I feel so very thankful for the life this man has given me.

"God keep you safe son," he says gruffly. And now I can see in his eyes that I have made him proud. My mother loops her arm into Edward's, and they step back and leave me space to say my goodbyes to my wife and children and then they are all gone. The train is packed full, but I find a space to squeeze down into. I am afraid now that the moment is nearing, but also strangely calm.

I do not go blindly into battle like the warriors of old. I have seen the blood and destruction of war through too many familiar eyes. I have seen the shadow that war casts in its wake. And yet I still go, simply because I know I must. Now that that realisation has come, there is no turning back.

But I am no fool. I know that this war like the last will take the best and the worst of us. It will strike at rich and poor indiscriminately, no respecter of class – this egalitarian monster will eat its way across Europe leaving no one untouched. It will steal our loved ones and make widows and orphans of us all. I march toward it softly, the dull jolt of the locomotive, pulling me, and thousands like me, to the fight and many thereafter to their graves. But not me, please God, not me.

I close my eyes and hear the music begin to whisper just as sleep threatens to take me. *Lacrimosa, Lacrimosa*, I am suddenly awake, but keep my eyes tight shut, lest I should lose this sight. I can see her fingers running across the keys with all the skill and grace that no poor man's child should muster. And I think of my long dead sister, Rose, who was no ordinary child. *Lacrimosa, Lacrimosa*, and my heart is full.

Footnote

1 This extract was part of a palace press statement released on behalf of King George V on the 7th of November 1919. It was later published in the *Times Newspaper*.

ABOUT THE AUTHOR

Km Bailey

KM Bailey grew up in the pretty village of Haddenham, Buckinghamshire, attending secondary school in the town of Aylesbury. As a child she was exposed to a wide range of classic and contemporary literature inspired by her grandfather Tom who shared his passion for music, books and poetry with all his grandchildren. From an early age she enjoyed acting and after completing a degree in English and Drama at London University went on to drama school, going on to enjoy the life of a jobbing actor around the UK. It was a life filled with fun, travel, excitement, grease paint and good company and despite the hand-to-mouth nature of the work she loved every minute of it.

After meeting her husband and starting a family, Kirstie, after several years working for a theatre publisher, moved to Scotland. She now lives in rural Perthshire and having retrained, works as a part-time teacher in a local primary school whilst combining this with her love of writing stories.

NOTE OF THANKS
I would like to thank Richard Vize for the use of the author's photo.

Printed in Great Britain
by Amazon